Fairy Tales; Their Origin and Meaning

John Thackray Bunce

Table of Contents

Fairy Tales; Their Origin and Meaning

John Thackray Bunce

FAIRY TALES, THEIR ORIGIN AND MEANING

With Some Account of Dwellers in Fairyland

BY

JOHN THACKRAY BUNCE

INTRODUCTORY NOTE.

The substance of this volume was delivered as a course of Christmas Holiday Lectures, in 1877, at the Birmingham and Midland Institute, of which the author was then the senior Vice–president. It was found that both the subject and the matter interested young people; and it was therefore thought that, revised and extended, the Lectures might not prove unacceptable in the form of a Book. The volume does not pretend to scientific method, or to complete treatment of the subject. Its aim is a very modest one: to furnish an inducement rather than a formal introduction to the study of Folk Lore; a study which, when once begun, the reader will pursue, with unflagging interest, in such works as the various writings of Mr. Max–Muller; the "Mythology of the Aryan Nations," by Mr. Cox; Mr. Ralston's "Russian Folk Tales;" Mr. Kelly's "Curiosities of Indo–European Folk Lore;" the Introduction to Mr. Campbell's "Popular Tales of the West Highlands," and other publications, both English and German, bearing upon the same subject. In the hope that his labour may serve this purpose, the author ventures to ask for an indulgent rather than a critical reception of this little volume.

BIRMINGHAM,
September, 1878.

CHAPTER I. ORIGIN OF FAIRY STORIES.

We are going into Fairy Land for a little while, to see what we can find there to amuse and instruct us this Christmas time. Does anybody know the way? There are no maps or guidebooks, and the places we meet with in our workaday world do not seem like the homes of the Fairies. Yet we have only to put on our Wishing Caps, and we can get into Fairy Land in a moment. The house–walls fade away, the winter sky brightens, the sun shines out, the weather grows warm and pleasant; flowers spring up, great trees cast a friendly shade, streams murmur cheerfully over their pebbly beds, jewelled fruits are to be had for the trouble of gathering them; invisible hands set out well–covered dinner–tables, brilliant and graceful forms flit in and out across our path, and we all at once find ourselves in the midst of a company of dear old friends whom we have known and loved ever since we knew anything. There is Fortunatus with his magic purse, and the square of carpet that carries him anywhere; and Aladdin with his wonderful lamp; and Sindbad with the diamonds he has picked up in the Valley of Serpents; and the Invisible Prince, who uses the fairy cat to get his dinner for him; and the Sleeping Beauty in the Wood, just awakened by the young Prince, after her long sleep of a hundred years; and Puss in Boots curling his whiskers after having eaten up the ogre who foolishly changed himself into a mouse; and Beauty and the Beast; and the Blue Bird; and Little Red Riding Hood, and Jack the Giant Killer, and Jack and the Bean Stalk; and the Yellow Dwarf; and Cinderella and her fairy godmother; and great numbers besides, of whom we haven't time to say anything now.

Fairy Tales; Their Origin and Meaning

And when we come to look about us, we see that there are other dwellers in Fairy Land; giants and dwarfs, dragons and griffins, ogres with great white teeth, and wearing seven–leagued boots; and enchanters and magicians, who can change themselves into any forms they please, and can turn other people into stone. And there are beasts and birds who can talk, and fishes that come out on dry land, with golden rings in their mouths; and good maidens who drop rubies and pearls when they speak, and bad ones out of whose mouths come all kinds of ugly things. Then there are evil–minded fairies, who always want to be doing mischief; and there are good fairies, beautifully dressed, and with shining golden hair and bright blue eyes and jewelled coronets, and with magic wands in their hands, who go about watching the bad fairies, and always come just in time to drive them away, and so prevent them from doing harm—the sort of Fairies you see once a year at the pantomimes, only more beautiful, and more handsomely dressed, and more graceful in shape, and not so fat, and who do not paint their faces, which is a bad thing for any woman to do, whether fairy or mortal.

Altogether, this Fairy Land that we can make for ourselves in a moment, is a very pleasant and most delightful place, and one which all of us, young and old, may well desire to get into, even if we have to come back from it sooner than we like. It is just the country to suit everybody, for all of us can find in it whatever pleases him best. If he likes work, there is plenty of adventure; he can climb up mountains of steel, or travel over seas of glass, or engage in single combat with a giant, or dive down into the caves of the little red dwarfs and bring up their hidden treasures, or mount a horse that goes more swiftly than the wind, or go off on a long journey to find the water of youth and life, or do anything else that happens to be very dangerous and troublesome. If he doesn't like work, it is again just the place to suit idle people, because it is all Midsummer holidays. I never heard of a school in Fairy Land, nor of masters with canes or birch rods, nor of impositions and long lessons to be learned when one gets home in the evening. Then the weather is so delightful. It is perpetual sunshine, so that you may lie out in the fields all day without catching cold; and yet it is not too hot, the sunshine being a sort of twilight, in which you see everything, quite clearly, but softly, and with beautiful colours, as if you were in a delightful dream.

And this goes on night and day, or at least what we call night, for they don't burn gas there, or candles, or anything of that kind; so that there is no regular going to bed and getting up; you just lie down anywhere when you want to rest, and when you have rested, you wake up again, and go on with your travels. There is one capital thing about Fairy

Land. There are no doctors there; not one in the whole country. Consequently nobody is ill, and there are no pills or powders, or brimstone and treacle, or senna tea, or being kept at home when you want to go out, or being obliged to go to bed early and have gruel instead of cake and sweetmeats. They don't want the doctors, because if you cut your finger it gets well directly, and even when people are killed, or are turned into stones, or when anything else unpleasant happens, it can all be put right in a minute or two. All you have to do when you are in trouble is to go and look for some wrinkled old woman in a patched old brown cloak, and be very civil to her, and to do cheerfully and kindly any service she asks of you, and then she will throw off the dark cloak, and become a young and beautiful Fairy Queen, and wave her magic wand, and everything will fall out just as you would like to have it.

As to Time, they take no note of it in Fairy Land. The Princess falls asleep for a hundred years, and wakes up quite rosy, and young, and beautiful. Friends and sweethearts are parted for years, and nobody seems to think they have grown older when they meet, or that life has become shorter, and so they fall to their youthful talk as if nothing had happened. Thus the dwellers in Fairy Land have no cares about chronology. With them there is no past or future; it is all present—so there are no disagreeable dates to learn, nor tables of kings, and when they reigned, or who succeeded them, or what battles they fought, or anything of that kind. Indeed there are no such facts to be learned, for when kings are wicked in Fairy Land, a powerful magician comes and twists their heads off, or puts them to death somehow; and when they are good kings they seem to live for ever, and always to be wearing rich robes and royal golden crowns, and to be entertaining Fairy Queens, and receiving handsome brilliant gifts from everybody who knows them.

Now this is Fairy Land, the dear sweet land of Once Upon a Time, where there is constant light, and summer days, and everlasting flowers, and pleasant fields and streams, and long dreams without rough waking, and ease of life, and all things strange and beautiful; where nobody wonders at anything that may happen; where good fairies are ever on the watch to help those whom they love; where youth abides, and there is no pain or death, and all trouble fades away, and whatever seems hard is made easy, and all things that look wrong come right in the end, and truth and goodness have their perpetual triumph, and the world is ever young.

And Fairy Land is always the same, and always has been, whether it is close to us—so close that we may enter it in a moment—or whether it is far off; in the stories that have come to us from the most ancient days, and the most distant lands, and in those which kind and clever story–tellers write for us now. It is the same in the legends of the mysterious East, as old as the beginning of life; the same in the glowing South, in the myths of ancient Greece; the same in the frozen regions of the Scandinavian North, and in the forests of the great Teuton land, and in the Islands of the West; the same in the tales that nurses tell to the little ones by the fireside on winter evenings, and in the songs that mothers sing to hush their babes to sleep; the same in the delightful folk–lore that Grimm has collected for us, and that dear Hans Andersen has but just ceased to tell.

All the chief stories that we know so well are to be found in all times, and in almost all countries. Cinderella, for one, is told in the language of every country in Europe, and the same legend is found in the fanciful tales related by the Greek poets; and still further back, it appears in very ancient Hindu legends. So, again, does Beauty and the Beast, so does our own familiar tale of Jack the Giant Killer, so also do a great number of other fairy stories, each being told in different countries and in different periods, with so much likeness as to show that all the versions came from the same source, and yet with so much difference as to show that none of the versions are directly copied from each other. Indeed, when we compare the myths and legends of one country with another, and of one period with another, we find out how they have come to be so much alike, and yet in some things so different. We see that there must have been one origin for all these stories, that they must have been invented by one people, that this people must have been afterwards divided, and that each part or division of it must have brought into its new home the legends once common to them all, and must have shaped and altered these according, to the kind of places in which they came to live: those of the North being sterner and more terrible, those of the South softer and fuller of light and colour, and adorned with touches of more delicate fancy. And this, indeed, is really the case. All the chief stories and legends are alike, because they were first made by one people; and all the nations in which they are now told in one form or another tell them because they are all descended from this one common stock. If you travel amongst them, or talk to them, or read their history, and learn their languages, the nations of Europe seem to be altogether unlike each other; they have different speech and manners, and ways of thinking, and forms of government, and even different looks—for you can tell them from one another by some peculiarity of appearance. Yet, in fact, all these nations belong to one great family—English, and German, and Russian, and French, and Italian, and Spanish, the nations of the North, and the South, and the West, and partly of the East of Europe, all came from one stock; and so did the Romans and Greeks who went before them; and so also did the Medes and Persians, and the Hindus, and some other peoples who have always remained in Asia. And to the people from whom all these nations have sprung learned men have given two names. Sometimes they are called the Indo–Germanic or Indo–European race, to show how widely they extend; and sometimes they are called the Aryan race, from a word which is found in their language, and which comes from the root "ar," to plough, and is supposed to mean noble, or of a good family.

But how do we know that there were any such people, and that we in England are descended from them, or that they were the forefathers of the other nations of Europe, and of the Hindus, and of the old Greeks and Romans? We know it by a most curious and ingenious process of what may be called digging out and building up. Some of you may remember that years ago there was found in New Zealand a strange–looking bone, which nobody could make anything of, and which seemed to have belonged to some creature quite lost to the world as we know it. This bone was sent home to England to a great naturalist, Professor Owen, of the British Museum, who looked at it, turned it over, thought about it, and then came to the conclusion that it was a bone which had once formed part of a gigantic bird. Then; by degrees, he began to see the kind of general form which such a bird must have presented, and finally, putting one thing to another, and fitting part to part, he declared it to be a bird of gigantic size, and of a particular character, which he was able to describe; and this opinion was confirmed by later discoveries of other bones and fragments, so that an almost complete skeleton of the Dinornis may now be seen in this country. Well, our knowledge of the Aryan people, and of our own descent from them, has been found out in much the same way. Learned men observed, as a curious thing, that in various European languages there were words of the same kind, and having the same root forms; they found also that these forms of roots existed in the older language of Greece; and then they found that they existed also in Sanskrit, the oldest language of India—that in which the sacred books of the Hindus are written. They discovered, further, that these words and their roots meant always the same things, and this led to the natural belief that they came from the same source. Then, by closer inquiry into the *Vedas*, or Hindu sacred books, another discovery was made, namely, that while the Sanskrit has preserved the words of the original language in their most primitive or earliest state, the other languages derived from the same source have kept some forms plainly coming from the same roots, but which Sanskrit has lost. Thus we are carried back to a language older than Sanskrit, and of which this is only one of the forms, and from this we know that there was a people which used a common tongue; and if different forms of this common tongue are found in India, in Persia, and throughout

Europe, we know that the races which inhabit these countries must, at sometime, have parted from the parent stock, and must have carried their language and their traditions along with them. So, to find out who these people were, we have to go back to the sacred books of the Hindus and the Persians, and to pick out whatever facts may be found there, and thus to build up the memorial of the Aryan race, just as Professor Owen built up the great New Zealand bird.

It would take too long, and would be much too dry, to show how this process has been completed step by step, and bit by bit. That belongs to a study called comparative philology, and to another called comparative mythology—that is, the studies of words and of myths, or legends—which some of those who read these pages may pursue with interest in after years. All that need be done now is to bring together such accounts of the Aryan people, our forefathers, as may be gathered from the writings of the learned men who have made this a subject of inquiry, and especially from the works of German and French writers, and more particularly from those of Mr. Max Muller, an eminent German, who lives amongst us in England, who writes in English, and who has done more, perhaps, than anybody else, to tell us what we know about this matter.

As to when the Aryans lived we know nothing, but that it was thousands of years ago, long before history began. As to the kind of people they were we know nothing in a direct way. They have left no traces of themselves in buildings, or weapons, or enduring records of any kind. There are no ruins of their temples or tombs, no pottery—which often helps to throw light upon ancient peoples–no carvings upon rocks or stones. It is only by the remains of their language that we can trace them; and we do this through the sacred books of the Hindus and Persians–the *Vedas* and the *Zend Avesta*—in which remains of their language are found, and by means of which, therefore, we get to know something about their dwelling–place, their manners, their customs, their religion, and their legends—the source and origin of our Fairy Tales.

In the *Zend Avesta*—the oldest sacred book of the Persians—or in such fragments of it as are left, there are sixteen countries spoken of as having been given by Ormuzd, the Good Deity, for the Aryans to live in; and these countries are described as a land of delight, which was turned, by Ahriman, the Evil Deity, into a land of death and cold; partly, it is said, by a great flood, which is described as being like Noah's flood recorded in the Book of Genesis. This land, as nearly as we can make it out, seems to have been the high, central district of Asia, to the north and west of the great chain of mountains of the Hindu

7

Koush, which form the frontier barrier of the present country of the Afghans. It stretched, probably, from the sources of the river Oxus to the shores of the Caspian Sea; and when the Aryans moved from their home, it is thought that the easterly portion of the tribes were those who marched southwards into India and Persia, and that those who were nearest the Caspian Sea marched westwards into Europe. It is not supposed that they were all one united people, but rather a number of tribes, having a common origin—though what was this original stock is quite beyond any knowledge we have, or even beyond our powers of conjecture. But, though the Aryan peoples were divided into tribes, and were spread over a tract of country nearly as large as half Europe, we may properly describe them generally, for so far as our knowledge goes, all the tribes had the same character.

They were a pastoral people—that is, their chief work was to look after their herds of cattle and to till the earth. Of this we find proof in the words and roots remaining of their language. From the same source, also, we know that they lived in dwellings built with wood and stone; that these dwellings were grouped together in villages; that they were fenced in against enemies, and that enclosures were formed to keep the cattle from straying, and that roads of some kind were made from one village to another. These things show that the Aryans had some claim to the name they took, and that in comparison with their forefathers, or with the savage or wandering tribes they knew, they had a right to call themselves respectable, excellent, honourable, masters, heroes—for all these are given as probable meanings of their name. Their progress was shown in another way. The rudest and earliest tribes of men used weapons of flint, roughly shaped into axes and spear–heads, or other cutting implements, with which they defended themselves in conflict, or killed the beasts of chase, or dug up the roots on which they lived. The Aryans were far in advance of this condition. They did not, it is believed, know the use of iron, but they knew and used gold, silver, and copper; they made weapons and other implements of bronze; they had ploughs to till the ground, and axes, and probably saws, for the purpose of cutting and shaping timber. Of pottery and weaving they knew something: the western tribes certainly used hemp and flax as materials for weaving, and when the stuff was woven the women made it into garments by the use of the needle. Thus we get a certain division of trades or occupations. There were the tiller of the soil, the herdsman, the smith who forged the tools and weapons of bronze, the joiner or carpenter who built the houses, and the weaver who made the clothing required for protection against a climate which was usually cold. Then there was also the boat–builder, for the Aryans had boats, though moved only by oars. There was yet

8

another class, the makers of personal ornaments, for these people had rings, bracelets, and necklaces made of the precious metals.

Of trade the Aryans knew something; but they had no coined money—all the trade was done by exchange of one kind of cattle, or grain or goods, for another. They had regulations as to property, their laws punished crime with fine, imprisonment, or death, just as ours do. They seem to have been careful to keep their liberties, the families being formed into groups, and these into tribes or clans, under the rule of an elected chief, while it is probable that a Great Chief or King ruled over several tribes and led them to war, or saw that the laws were put into force.

Now we begin to see something of these ancient forefathers of ours, and to understand what kind of people they were. Presently we shall have to look into their religion, out of which our Fairy Stories were really made; but first, there are one or two other things to be said about them. One of these shows that they were far in advance of savage races, for they could count as high as one hundred, while savages can seldom get further than the number of their fingers; and they had also advanced so far as to divide the year into twelve months, which they took from the changes of the moon. Then their family relations were very close and tender. "Names were given to the members of families related by marriage as well as by blood. A welcome greeted the birth of children, as of those who brought joy to the home; and the love that should be felt between brother and sister was shown in the names given to them: *bhratar* (or brother) being he who sustains or helps; *svasar* (or sister) she who pleases or consoles. The daughter of each household was called *duhitar,* from *duh*, a root which in Sanskrit means to milk, by which we know that the girls in those days were the milking–maids. Father comes from a root, *pa*, which means to protect or support; mother, *matar*, has the meaning of maker."[1]

Now we may sum up what we know of this ancient people and their ways; and we find in them much that is to be found in their descendants—the love of parents and children, the closeness of family ties, the protection of life and property, the maintenance of law and order, and, as we shall see presently, a great reverence for *God*. Also, they were well versed in the arts of life—they built houses, formed villages or towns, made roads, cultivated the soil, raised great herds of cattle and other animals; they made boats and land–carriages, worked in metals for use and ornament, carried on trade with each other, knew how to count, and were able to divide their time so as to reckon by months and days as well as by seasons. Besides all this, they had something more and of still higher

9

value, for the fragments of their ancient poems or hymns preserved in the Hindu and Persian sacred books show that they thought much of the spirit of man as well as of his bodily life; that they looked upon sin as an evil to be punished or forgiven by the Gods, that they believed in a life after the death of the body, and that they had a strong feeling for natural beauty and a love of searching into the wonders of the earth and of the heavens.

The religion of the Aryan races, in its beginning, was a very simple and a very noble one. They looked up to the heavens and saw the bright sun, and the light and beauty and glory of the day. They saw the day fade into night and the clouds draw themselves across the sky, and then they saw the dawn and the light and life of another day. Seeing these things, they felt that some Power higher than man ordered and guided them; and to this great Power they gave the name of *Dyaus*, from a root-word which means "to shine." And when, out of the forces and forms of Nature, they afterwards fashioned other Gods, this name of Dyaus became *Dyaus pitar*, the Heaven-Father, or Lord of All; and in far later times, when the western Aryans had found their home in Europe, the *Dyaus pitar* of the central Asian land became the Zeupater of the Greeks, and the Jupiter of the Romans; and the first part of his name gave us the word Deity, which we apply to *God*. So, as Professor Max Muller tells us, the descendants of the ancient Aryans, "when they search for a name for what is most exalted and yet most dear to every one of us, when they wish to express both awe and love, the infinite and the finite, they can do but what their old fathers did when gazing up to the eternal sky, and feeling the presence of a Being as far as far, and as near as near can be; they can but combine the self-same words and utter once more the primeval Aryan prayer, Heaven-Father, in that form which will endure for ever, 'Our Father, which art in Heaven.'"

The feeling which the Aryans had towards the Heaven-Father is very finely shown in one of the oldest hymns in the *Rig Veda*, or the Book of Praise—a hymn written 4,000 years ago, and addressed to Varuna, or the All-Surrounder, the ancient Hindu name for the chief deity:—

"Let me not, O Varuna, enter into the house of clay.
  Have mercy! Almighty, have mercy!
If I go trembling, like a cloud driven by the wind,
  Have mercy! Almighty, have mercy!
Through want of strength, thou strong and bright God,

10

have I gone wrong;
Have mercy! Almighty, have mercy!"

But, besides Dyaus pitar, or Varuna, the Aryans worshipped other gods, whom they made for themselves out of the elements, and the changes of night and day, and the succession of the seasons. They worshipped the sky, the earth, the sun, the dawn, fire, water, and wind. The chief of these deities were Agni, the fire; Prithivi, the earth; Ushas, the dawn; Mitra, or Surya, the sun; Indra, the sky; Maruts, the storm–winds; and Varuna, the All–Surrounder. To these deities sacrifice was offered and prayer addressed; but they had no priests or temples—these came in later ages, when men thought they had need of others to stand between them and *God*. But the ancient Aryans saw the Deity everywhere, and stood face to face with Him in Nature. He was to them the early morning, the brightness of midday, the gloom of evening, the darkness of night, the flash of the lightning, the roll of the thunder, and the rush of the mighty storm–wind. It seems strange to us that those who could imagine the one Heaven–Father should degrade Him by making a multitude of Gods; but this came easily to them, partly out of a desire to account for all they saw in Nature, and which their fancy clothed in divine forms, and partly out of reverence for the great All Father, by filling up the space between Him and themselves with inferior Gods, all helping to make His greatness the greater and His power the mightier.

We cannot look into this old religion of the Aryans any further, because our business is to see how their legends are connected with the myths and stories which are spread by their descendants over a great part of East and West. Now this came about in the way we are going to describe.

The mind of the Aryan peoples in their ancient home was full of imagination. They never ceased to wonder at what they heard and saw in the sky and upon the earth. Their language was highly figurative, and so the things which struck them with wonder, and which they could not explain, were described under forms and names which were familiar to them. Thus the thunder was to them the bellowing of a mighty beast or the rolling of a great chariot. In the lightning they saw a brilliant serpent, or a spear shot across the sky, or a great fish darting swiftly through the sea of cloud. The clouds were heavenly cows, who shed milk upon the earth and refreshed it; or they were webs woven by heavenly women, who drew water from the fountains on high and poured it down as rain. The sun was a radiant wheel, or a golden bird, or an eye, or a shining egg, or a horse

11

of matchless speed, or a slayer of the cloud–dragons. Sometimes it was a frog, when it seemed to be sinking into or squatting upon the water; and out of this fancy, when the meaning of it was lost, there grew a Sanskrit legend, which is to be found also in Teutonic and Celtic myths. This story is, that Bheki (the frog) was a lovely maiden who was found by a king, who asked her to be his wife. So she married him, but only on condition that he should never show her a drop of water. One day she grew tired, and asked for water. The king gave it to her, and she sank out of his sight; in other words, the sun disappears when it touches the water.

This imagery of the Aryans was applied by them to all they saw in the sky. Sometimes, as we have said, the clouds were cows; they were also dragons, which sought to slay the sun; or great ships floating across the sky, and casting anchor upon earth; or rocks, or mountains, or deep caverns, in which evil deities hid the golden light. Then, also, they were shaped by fancy into animals of various kinds–the bear, the wolf, the dog, the ox; and into giant birds, and into monsters which were both bird and beast.

The Winds, again, in their fancy, were the companions or the ministers of Indra, the sky–god. The Maruts, or spirits of the winds, gathered into their host the souls of the dead—thus giving birth to the Scandinavian and Teutonic legend of the Wild Horseman, who rides at midnight through the stormy sky, with his long train of dead behind him, and his weird hounds before. The Ribhus, or Arbhus, again, were the sunbeams or the lightning, who forged the armour of the Gods, and made their thunderbolts, and turned old people young, and restored out of the hide alone the slaughtered cow on which the Gods had feasted. Out of these heavenly artificers, the workers of the clouds, there came, in later times, two of the most striking stories of ancient legend—that of Thor, the Scandinavian thunder–god, who feasted at night on the goats which drew his chariot, and in the morning, by a touch of his hammer, brought them back to life; and that of Orpheus in the beautiful Greek legend, the master of divine song, who moved the streams, and rocks, and trees, by the beauty of his music, and brought back his wife Eurydike from the shades of death. In our Western fairy tales we still have these Ribhus, or Arbhus, transformed, through various changes of language, into Albs, and Elfen, and last into our English Elves. It is not needful to go further into the fanciful way in which the old Aryans slowly made ever–increasing deities and superhuman beings for themselves out of all the forms and aspects of Nature; or how their Hindu and Persian and Greek and Teuton descendants peopled all earth, and air, and sky, and water, with good and bad spirits and imaginary powers. But, as we shall see later, all these creatures grew out of one thing

12

only—the Sun, and his influence upon the earth. Aryan myths were no more than poetic fancies about light and darkness, cloud and rain, night and day, storm and wind; and when they moved westward and southward, the Aryan races brought these legends with them; and they were shaped by degrees into the innumerable gods and demons of the Hindus, the divs and jinns of the Persians, the great gods, the minor deities, and nymphs, and fauns, and satyrs of Greek mythology and poetry; the stormy divinities, the giants, and trolls of the cold and rugged North; the dwarfs of the German forests; the elves who dance merrily in the moonlight of an English summer; and the "good people" who play mischievous tricks upon stray peasants amongst the Irish hills. Almost all, indeed, that we have of a legendary kind comes to us from our Aryan forefathers; sometimes scarcely changed, sometimes so altered that we have to puzzle out the links between the old and the new; but all these myths and traditions, and Old-world stories, when we come to know the meaning of them, take us back to the time when the Aryan races dwelt together in the high lands of Central Asia, and they all mean the same things—that is, the relation between the sun and the earth, the succession of night and day, of winter and summer, of storm and calm, of cloud and tempest, and golden sunshine and bright blue sky. And this is the source from which we get our Fairy Stories; for underneath all of them there are the same fanciful meanings, only changed and altered in the way of putting them, by the lapse of ages of time, by the circumstances of different countries, and by the fancy of those who kept the wonderful tales alive without knowing what they meant.

When the change happened that brought about all this, we do not know. It was thousands of years ago that the Aryan people began their march out of their old country in mid-Asia. But from the remains of their language and the likeness of their legends to those amongst other nations, we do know that ages and ages ago their country grew too small for them, so they were obliged to move away from it. They could not go eastward, for the great mountains shut them in; they could not go northward, for the great desert was too barren for their flocks and herds. So they turned, some of them southward into India and Persia, and some of them westward into Europe—at the time, perhaps, when the land of Europe stretched from the borders of Asia to our own islands, and when there was no sea between us and what is now the mainland. How they made their long and toilsome march we know not. But, as Kingsley writes of such a movement of an ancient tribe, so we may fancy these old Aryans marching westward—"the tall, bare-limbed men, with stone axes on their shoulders and horn bows at their backs, with herds of grey cattle, guarded by huge lop-eared mastiffs, with shaggy white horses, heavy-horned sheep and silky goats, moving always westward through the boundless steppes, whither or why we know not, but that the All—Father had sent them forth. And behind us [he makes them say] the rosy snow—peaks died into ghastly grey, lower and lower, as every evening came; and before us the plains spread infinite, with gleaming salt—lakes, and ever—fresh tribes of gaudy flowers. Behind us, dark: lines of living beings streamed down the mountain slopes; around us, dark lines crawled along the plains—westward, westward ever. Who could stand against us? We met the wild asses on the steppe, and tamed them, and made them our slaves. We slew the bison herds, and swam broad rivers on their skins. The Python snake lay across our path; the wolves and wild dogs snarled at us out of their coverts; we slew them and went on. The forests rose in black tangled barriers, we hewed our way through them and went on. Strange giant tribes met us, and eagle—visaged hordes, fierce and foolish; we smote them, hip and thigh, and went on, west—ward ever." And so, as they went on, straight towards the west, or as they turned north and south, and thus overspread new lands, they brought with them their old ways of thought and forms of belief, and the stories in which these had taken form; and on these were built up the Gods and Heroes, and all wonder—working creatures and things, and the poetical fables and fancies which have come down to us, and which still linger in our customs and our Fairy Tales bright and sunny and many coloured in the warm regions of the south; sterner and wilder and rougher in the north; more homelike in the middle and western countries; but always alike in their main features, and always having the same meaning when we come to dig it out; and these forms and this meaning being the same in the lands of the Western Aryans as in those still peopled by the Aryans of the East.

It would take a very great book to give many examples of the myths and stories which are alike in all the Aryan countries; but we may see by one instance what the likeness is; and it shall be a story which all will know when they read it.

Once upon a time there was a Hindu Rajah, who had an only daughter, who was born with a golden necklace. In this necklace was her soul; and if the necklace were taken off and worn by some one else, the Princess would die. On one of her birthdays the Rajah gave his daughter a pair of slippers with ornaments of gold and gems upon them. The Princess went out upon a mountain to pluck the flowers that grew there, and while she was stooping to pluck them one of her slippers came off and fell down into a forest below. A Prince, who was hunting in the forest, picked up the lost slipper, and was so charmed with it that he desired to make its owner his wife. So he made his wish known everywhere, but nobody came to claim the slipper, and the poor Prince grew very sad. At last some people from the Rajah's country heard of it, and told the Prince where to find

14

the Rajah's daughter; and he went there, and asked for her as his wife, and they were married. Sometime after, another wife of the Prince, being jealous of the Rajah's daughter, stole her necklace, and put it on her own neck, and then the Rajah's daughter died. But her body did not decay, nor did her face lose its bloom; and the Prince went every day to see her, for he loved her very much although she was dead. Then he found out the secret of the necklace, and got it back again, and put it on his dead wife's neck, and her soul was born again in her, and she came back to life, and they lived happy ever after.

This Hindu story of the lost slipper is met with again in a legend of the ancient Greeks, which tells that while a beautiful woman, named Rhodope—or the rosy–cheeked—was bathing, an eagle picked up one of her slippers and flew away with it, and carried it off to Egypt, and dropped it in the lap of the King of that country, as he sat at Memphis on the judgment–seat. The slipper was so small and beautiful that the King fell in love with the wearer of it, and had her sought for, and when she was found he made her his wife. Another story of the same kind. It is found in many countries, in various forms, and is that of Cinderella, the poor neglected maiden, whom her stepmother set to work in the kitchen, while her sisters went to the grand balls and feasts at the King's palace. You know how Cinderella's fairy godmother came and dressed her like a princess, and sent her to the ball; how the King's son fell in love with her; how she lost one of her slippers, which the Prince picked up; how he vowed that he would marry the maiden who could fit on the lost slipper; how all the ladies of the court tried to do it, and failed, Cinderella's sisters amongst them; and how Cinderella herself put on the slipper, produced the fellow to it, was married to the King's son, and lived happily with him.

Now the story of Cinderella helps us to find out the meaning of our Fairy Tales; and takes us back straight to the far–off land where fairy legends began, and to the people who made them. Cinderella, and Rhodope, and the Hindu Rajah's daughter, and the like, are but different forms of the same ancient myth. It is the story of the Sun and the Dawn. Cinderella, grey and dark, and dull, is all neglected when she is away from the Sun, obscured by the envious Clouds her sisters, and by her stepmother the Night. So she is Aurora, the Dawn, and the fairy Prince is the Morning Sun, ever pursuing her, to claim her for his bride. This is the legend as we find it in the ancient Hindu sacred books; and this explains at once the source and the meaning of the Fairy Tale.

Nor is it in the story of Cinderella alone that we trace the ancient Hindu legends. There is scarcely a tale of Greek or Roman mythology, no legend of Teutonic or Celtic or Scandinavian growth, no great romance of what we call the middle ages, no fairy story taken down from the lips of ancient folk, and dressed for us in modern shape and tongue, that we do not find, in some form or another, in these Eastern poems. The Greek gods are there—Zeus, the Heaven–Father, and his wife Hera, "and Phoebus Apollo the Sun–god, and Pallas Athene, who taught men wisdom and useful arts, and Aphrodite the Queen of Beauty, and Poseidon the Ruler of the Sea, and Hephaistos the King of the Fire, who taught men to work in metals."[2] There, too, are legends which resemble those of Orpheus and Eurydike, of Eros and Psyche, of Jason and the Golden Fleece, of the labours of Herakles, of Sigurd and Brynhilt, of Arthur and the Knights of the Round Table. There, too, in forms which can be traced with ease, we have the stories of Fairyland—the germs of the Thousand and One Tales of the Arabian Nights, the narratives of giants, and dwarfs, and enchanters; of men and maidens transformed by magic arts into beasts and birds; of riches hidden in the caves and bowels of the earth, and guarded by trolls and gnomes; of blessed lands where all is bright and sunny, and where there is neither work nor care. Whatever, indeed, is strange or fanciful, or takes us straight from our grey, hard–working world into the sweet and peaceful country of Once Upon a Time, is to be found in these ancient Hindu books, and is repeated, from the source whence they were drawn, in many countries of the East and West; for the people whose traditions the Vedas record were the forefathers of those who now dwell in India, in Persia, in the border–lands, and in most parts of Europe. Yes; strange as it may seem, all of us, who differ so much in language, in looks in customs and ways of thought, in all that marks out one nation from another—all of us have a common origin and a common kindred. Greek and Roman, and Teuton and Kelt and Slav, ancient and modern, all came from the same stock. English and French, Spanish and Germans, Italians and Russians, all unlike in outward show, are linked together in race; and not only with each other, but also claim kindred with the people who now fill the fiery plains of India, and dwell on the banks of her mighty rivers, and on the slopes of her great mountain–chains, and who still recite the sacred books, and sing the ancient hymns from which the mythology of the West is in great part derived, whence our folk–lore comes, and which give life and colour and meaning to our legends of romance and our Tales of Fairyland.

By taking a number of stories containing the same idea, but related in different ages and in countries far away from each other, we shall see how this likeness of popular tradition runs through all of them, and shows their common origin. So we will go to the next chapter, and tell a few kindred tales from East and West, and South and North.

---

[1] Edward Clodd, *The Childhood of Religions: Embracing a Simple Account of the Birth and Growth of Myths and Legends*, p. 76–77. (1878)

[2] Kingsley's *Heroes*, preface, p. xv.

CHAPTER II. KINDRED TALES FROM DIVERS LANDS: EROS AND PSYCHE.

Once upon a time there lived a king and a queen, who had three beautiful daughters. The youngest of them, who was called Psyche, was the loveliest; she was so very beautiful that she was thought to be a second Aphrodite, the Goddess of Beauty and Love, and all who saw her worshipped her as if she were the goddess; so that the temples of Aphrodite were deserted and her worship neglected, and Psyche was preferred to her; and as she passed along the streets, or came into the temples, the people crowded round her, and scattered flowers under her feet, and offered garlands to her. Now, when Aphrodite knew this she grew very angry, and resolved to punish Psyche, so as to make her a wonder and a shame for ever. So Aphrodite sent for her son Eros, the God of Love, and took him to the city where Psyche lived, and showed the maiden to him, and bade him afflict her with love for a man who should be the most wicked and most miserable of mankind, an outcast, a beggar, one who had done some great wrong, and had fallen so low that no man in the whole world could be so wretched. Eros agreed that he would do what his mother wished; but this was only a pretence, for when he saw Psyche he fell in love with her himself, and made up his mind that she should be his own wife. The first thing to do was to get the maiden into his own care and to hide her from the vengeance of Aphrodite. So he put it into the mind of her father to go to the shrine of Phoebus, at Miletus, and ask the god what should be done with Psyche. The king did so, and he was bidden by an oracle to dress Psyche as a bride, to take her to the brow of a high mountain, and to leave her there, and that after a time a great monster would come and take her away and make her his wife. So Psyche was decked in bridal garments, was taken to a rock on the top of a mountain, and was left there as a sacrifice to turn away the wrath of Aphrodite. But Eros took care that she came to no harm. He went to Zephyrus, the God of the West Wind, and told him to carry Psyche gently down into a beautiful valley, and to lay her softly on the turf, amidst lovely flowers. So Zephyrus lulled Psyche to sleep, and then carried her safely down, and laid her in the place where Eros had bidden him. When Psyche awoke from sleep she saw a thick grove, with a crystal fountain in it, and close to the fountain there was a stately palace, fit for the dwelling of a king or a god. She went into the palace, and found it very wonderful. The walls and ceilings were made of cedar and ivory, there were golden columns holding up the roof, the floors were laid with precious stones, so put together as to make pictures, and on the walls were carvings in gold and silver of birds, and beasts, and flowers, and all kinds of strange and beautiful things. And there were also great treasure places full of gold, and silver, and gems, in such great measure that it seemed as if all the riches of the world were gathered there. But nowhere was there any living creature to be seen; all the palace was empty, and Psyche was there alone. And while she went trembling and fearing through the rooms, and wondering whose all this might be, she heard voices, as of invisible maidens, which told her that the palace was for her, and that they who spoke, but whom she might not see, were her servants. And the voices bade her go first to the bath, and then to a royal banquet which was prepared for her. So Psyche, still wondering, went to the bath, and then to a great and noble room, where there was a royal seat, and upon this she placed herself, and then unseen attendants put before her all kinds of delicate food and wine; and while she ate and drank there was a sound as of a great number of people singing the most charming music, and of one playing upon the lyre; but none of them could she see. Then night came on, and all the beautiful palace grew dark, and Psyche laid herself down upon a couch to sleep. Then a great terror fell upon her, for she heard footsteps, which came nearer and nearer, and she thought it was the monster whose bride the oracle of Phoebus had destined her to be. And the footsteps drew closer to her, and then an unseen being came to her couch and lay down beside her, and made her his wife; and he lay there until just before the break of day, and then he departed, and it was still so dark that Psyche could not see his form; nor did he speak, so that she could not guess from his voice what kind of creature it was to whom the Fates had wedded her. So Psyche lived for a long while, wandering about her palace in the daytime, tended by her unseen guardians, and every night her husband came to her and stayed until daybreak. Then she began to long to hear about her father and mother, and to see her sisters, and she begged leave of her husband that these might come to her for a time. To this Eros agreed, and gave her leave to give her sisters rich gifts, but warned her that she must answer no questions they might ask about him, and that she must not listen to any advice they might give her to find out who he was, or else a great misfortune would happen to her. Then Zephyrus brought the sisters of Psyche to her, and they stayed with her for a little while, and were very curious

18

to know who her husband was, and what he was like. But Psyche, mindful of the commands of Eros, put them off, first with one story and then with another, and at last sent them away, loaded with jewels. Now Psyche's sisters were envious of her, because such good fortune had not happened to themselves, to have such a grand palace, and such store of wealth, and they plotted between themselves to make her discover her husband, hoping to get some good for themselves out of it, and not caring what happened to her. And it so fell out that they had their way, for Psyche again getting tired of solitude, again begged of her husband that her sisters might come to see her once more, to which, with much sorrow, he consented, but warned her again that if she spoke of him, or sought to see him, all her happiness would vanish, and that she would have to bear a life of misery. But it was fated that Psyche should disobey her husband; and it fell out in this way. When her sisters came to her again they questioned her about her husband, and persuaded her that she was married to a monster too terrible to be looked at, and they told her that this was the reason why he never came in the daytime, and refused to let himself be seen at night. Then they also persuaded her that she ought to put an end to the enchantment by killing the monster; and for this purpose they gave her a sharp knife, and they gave her also a lamp, so that while he was asleep she might look at him, so as to know where to strike. Then, being left alone, poor Psyche's mind was full of terror, and she resolved to follow the advice of her sisters. So when her husband was asleep, she went and fetched the lamp, and looked at him by its light; and then she saw that, instead of a deadly monster, it was Eros himself, the God of Love, to whom she was married. But while she was filled with awe and delight at this discovery, the misfortune happened which Eros had foretold. A drop of oil from the lamp fell upon the shoulder of the god, and he sprang up from the couch, reproached Psyche for her fatal curiosity, and vanished from her sight; and then the beautiful palace vanished also, and Psyche found herself lying on the bare cold earth, weeping, deserted, and alone.

Then poor Psyche began a long and weary journey, to try to find the husband she had lost, but she could not, for he had gone to his mother Aphrodite, to be cured of his wound; and Aphrodite, finding out that Eros had fallen in love with Psyche, determined to punish her, and to prevent her from finding Eros. First Psyche went to the god Pan, but he could not help her; then she went to the goddess Demeter, the Earth-Mother, but she warned her against the vengeance of Aphrodite, and sent her away. And the great goddess Hera did the same; and at last, abandoned by every one, Psyche went to Aphrodite herself, and the goddess, who had caused great search to be made for her, now ordered her to be beaten and tormented, and then ridiculed her sorrows, and taunted her with the loss of Eros, and set her to work at many tasks that seemed impossible to be done. First the goddess took a great heap of seeds of wheat, barley, millet, poppy, lentils, and beans, and mixed them all together, and then bade Psyche separate them into their different kinds by nightfall. Now there were so many of them that this was impossible; but Eros, who pitied Psyche, though she had lost him, sent a great many ants, who parted the seeds from each other and arranged them in their proper heaps, so that by evening all that Aphrodite had commanded was done. Then the goddess was very angry, and fed Psyche on bread and water, and next day she set Psyche another task. This was to collect a quantity of golden wool from the sheep of the goddess, creatures so fierce and wild that no mortal could venture near them and escape with life. Then Psyche thought herself lost; but Pan came to her help and bade her wait until evening, when the golden sheep would be at rest, and then she might from the trees and shrubs collect all the wool she needed. So Psyche fulfilled this task also. But Aphrodite was still unsatisfied. She now demanded a crystal urn, filled with icy waters from the fountain of Oblivion. The fountain was placed on the summit of a great mountain; it issued from a fissure in a lofty rock, too steep for any one to ascend, and from thence it fell into a narrow channel, deep, winding, and rugged, and guarded on each side by terrible dragons, which never slept. And the rush of the waters, as they rolled along, resembled a human voice, always crying out to the adventurous explorer—"Beware! fly! or you perish!" Here Psyche thought her sufferings at an end; sooner than face the dragons and climb the rugged rocks she must die. But again Eros helped her, for he sent the eagle of Zeus, the All–Father, and the eagle took the crystal urn in his claws, flew past the dragons, settled on the rock, and drew the water of the black fountain, and gave it safely to Psyche, who carried it back and presented it to the angry Aphrodite. But the goddess, still determined that Psyche should perish, set her another task, the hardest and most dangerous of all. "Take this box," she said, "go with it into the infernal regions to Persephone, and ask her for a portion of her beauty, that I may adorn myself with it for the supper of the gods." Now on hearing this, poor Psyche knew that the goddess meant to destroy her; so she went up to a lofty tower, meaning to throw herself down headlong so that she might be killed, and thus pass into the realm of Hades, never to return. But the tower was an enchanted place, and a voice from it spoke to her and bade her be of good cheer, and told her what to do. She was to go to a city of Achaia and find near it a mountain, and in the mountain she would see a gap, from which a narrow road led straight into the infernal regions. But the voice warned her of many things which must be done on the journey, and of others which must be avoided. She was to take in each hand a piece of barley bread, soaked in honey, and in her mouth she was to put two pieces of money. On entering the dreary path she would meet an old man driving a lame ass, laden with wood, and the old man would ask her for help, but she was to pass him by in silence. Then she would come to the bank of the black river, over which the boatman Charon ferries the souls of the dead; and from her mouth Charon must take one piece of money, she saying not a word. In crossing the river a dead hand would stretch itself up to her, and a dead face, like that of her father, would appear, and a voice would issue from the dead man's mouth, begging for the other piece of money, that he might pay for his passage, and get released from the doom of floating for ever in the grim flood of Styx. But still she was to keep silence, and to let the dead man cry out in vain; for all these, the voice told her, were snares prepared by Aphrodite, to make her let go the money, and to let fall the pieces of bread. Then, at the gate of the palace of Persephone she would meet the great three–headed dog, Kerberos, who keeps watch there for ever, and to him, to quiet his terrible barking, she must give one piece of the bread, and pass on, still never speaking. So Kerberos would allow her to pass; but still another danger would await her. Persephone would greet her kindly, and ask her to sit upon soft cushions, and to eat of a fine banquet. But she must refuse both offers—sitting only on the ground, and eating only of the bread of mortals, or else she must remain for ever in the gloomy regions below the earth. Psyche listened to this counsel, and obeyed it. Everything happened as the voice had foretold. She saw the old man with the overladen ass, she permitted Charon to take the piece of money from her lips, she stopped her ears against the cry of the dead man floating in the black river, she gave the honey bread to Kerberos, and she refused the soft cushions and the banquet offered to her by the queen of the infernal regions. Then Persephone gave her the precious beauty demanded by Aphrodite, and shut it up in the box, and Psyche came safely back into the light of day, giving to Kerberos, the three–headed dog, the remaining piece of honey bread, and to Charon the remaining piece of money. But now she fell into a great danger. The voice in the tower had warned her not to look into the box; but she was tempted by a strong desire, and so she opened it, that she might see and use for herself the beauty of the gods. But when she opened the box it was empty, save of a vapour of sleep, which seized upon Psyche, and made her as if she were dead. In this unhappy state, brought upon her by the vengeance of Aphrodite, she would have been lost for ever, but Eros, healed of the wound caused by the burning oil, came himself to her help, roused her from the death–like sleep, and put her in a place of safety. Then Eros flew up into the abode of the gods, and besought Zeus to protect Psyche against his mother Aphrodite; and Zeus, calling an assembly of the gods, sent Hermes to bring Psyche thither, and then he declared her immortal, and she and Eros were wedded to each other; and there was a great feast in Olympus. And the sisters of Psyche, who had striven to ruin her, were punished for their crimes, for Eros appeared to them one after the other in a dream, and promised to make each of them his wife, in place of Psyche, and bade each throw herself from the great rock whence Psyche was carried into the beautiful valley by Zephyrus; and both the sisters did as the dream told them, and they were dashed to pieces, and perished miserably.

Now this is the story of Eros and Psyche, as it is told by Apuleius, in his book of *Metamorphoses*, written nearly two thousand years ago. But the story was told ages before Apuleius by people other than the Greeks, and in a language which existed long before theirs. It is the tale of Urvasi and Pururavas, which is to be found in one of the oldest of the Vedas, or Sanskrit sacred books, which contain the legends of the Aryan race before it broke up and went in great fragments southward into India, and westward into Persia and Europe. A translation of the story of Urvasi and Pururavas is given by Mr. Max−Muller,[3] who also tells what the story means, and this helps us to see the meaning of the tale of Eros and Psyche, and of many other myths which occur among all the branches of the Aryan family; among the Teutons, the Scandinavians, and the Slavs, as well as among the Greeks. Urvasi, then, was an immortal being, a kind of fairy, who fell in love with Pururavas, a hero and a king; and she married him, and lived with him, on this condition—that she should never see him unless he was dressed in his royal robes. Now there was a ewe, with two lambs, tied to the couch of Urvasi and Pururavas; and the fairies—or Gandharvas, as the kinsfolk of Urvasi were called—wished to get her back amongst them; and so they stole one of the lambs. Then Urvasi reproached her husband, and said, "They take away my darling, as if I lived in a land where there is no hero and no man." The fairies stole the other lamb, and Urvasi reproached her husband again, saying, "How can that be a land without heroes or men where I am?" Then Pururavas hastened to bring back the pet lamb; so eager was he that he stayed not to clothe himself, and so sprang up naked. Then the Gandharvas sent a flash of lightning, and Urvasi saw her husband naked as if by daylight; and then she cried out to her kinsfolk, "I come back," and she vanished. And Pururavas, made wretched by the loss of his love, sought her everywhere, and once he was permitted to see her, and when he saw her, he said he should die if she did not come back to him. But Urvasi could not return; but she gave him leave to come to her, on the last night of the year, to the golden seats; and he stayed with her for that night. And Urvasi said to him, "The Gandharvas will to−morrow grant thee a wish; choose." He said; "Choose thou for me." She replied, "Say to them, Let me be one of you." And he said this, and they taught him how to make the sacred fire, and he became one of them, and dwelt with Urvasi for ever.

Now this, we see, is like the story of Eros and Psyche; and Mr. Max–Muller teaches us what it means. It is the story of the Sun and the Dawn. Urvasi is the Dawn, which must vanish or die when it beholds the risen Sum; and Pururavas is the Sun; and they are united again at sunset, when the Sun dies away into night. So, in the Greek myth, Eros is the dawning Sun, and when Psyche, the Dawn, sees him, he flies from her, and it is only at nightfall that they can be again united. In the same paper Mr. Max–Muller shows how this root idea of the Aryan race is found again in another of the most beautiful of Greek myths or stories—that of Orpheus and Eurydike. In the Greek legends the Dawn has many names; one of them is Eurydike. The name of her husband, Orpheus, comes straight from the Sanskrit: it is the same as Ribhu or Arbhu, which is a name of Indra, or the Sun, or which may be used for the rays of the Sun. The old story, then, says our teacher, was this: "Eurydike (the Dawn) is bitten by a serpent (the Night); she dies, and descends into the lower regions. Orpheus follows her, and obtains from the gods that his wife should follow him, if he promised not to look back. Orpheus promises—ascends from the dark world below; Eurydike is behind him as he rises, but, drawn by doubt or by love, he looks round; the first ray of the Sun glances at the Dawn; and the Dawn fades away."

We have now seen that the Greek myth is like a much older myth existing amongst the Aryan race before it passed westward. We have but to look to other collections of Aryan folk–lore to find that in some of its features the legend is common to all branches of the Aryan family. In our own familiar story of "Beauty and the Beast," for instance, we have the same idea. There are the three sisters, one of whom is chosen as the bride of an enchanted monster, who dwells in a beautiful palace. By the arts of her sisters she is kept away from him, and he is at the point of death through his grief. Then she returns, and he revives, and becomes changed into a handsome Prince, and they live happy ever after. One feature of these legends is that beings closely united to each other—as closely, that is, as the Sun and the Dawn—may not look upon each other without misfortune. This is illustrated in the charming Scandinavian story of "The Land East of the Sun and West of the Moon," which is told in various forms; the best of them being in Mr. Morris's beautiful poem in "The Earthly Paradise," and in Dr. Dasent's Norse Tales.[4] We shall abridge Dr. Dasent's version, telling the story in our own way:

There was a poor peasant who had a large family whom he could scarcely keep; and there were several daughters amongst them. The loveliest was the youngest daughter; who was very beautiful indeed. One evening in autumn, in bad weather, the family sat round the fire; and there came three taps at the window. The father went out to see who it was, and he found only a great White Bear. And the White Bear said, "If you will give me your youngest daughter, I will make you rich." So the peasant went in and asked his daughter if she would be the wife of the White Bear; and the daughter said "No." So the White Bear went away, but said he would come back in a few days to see if the maiden had changed her mind. Now her father and mother talked to her so much about it, and seemed so anxious to be well off, that the maiden agreed to be the wife of the White Bear: and when he came again, she said "Yes," and the White Bear told her to sit upon his back, and hold by his shaggy coat, and away they went together. After the maiden had ridden for a long way, they came to a great hill, and the White Bear gave a knock on the hill with his paw, and the hill opened, and they went in. Now inside the hill there was a palace with fine rooms, ornamented with gold and silver, and all lighted up; and there was a table ready laid; and the White Bear gave the maiden a silver bell, and told her to ring it when she wanted anything. And when the maiden had eaten and drank, she went to bed, in a beautiful bed with silk pillows and curtains, and gold fringe to them. Then, in the dark, a man came and lay down beside her. This was the White Bear, who was an Enchanted Prince, and who was able to put off the shape of a beast at night, and to become a man again; but before daylight, he went away and turned once more into a White Bear, so that his wife could never see him in the human form. Well, this went on for some time, and the wife of the White Bear was very happy with her kind husband, in the beautiful palace he had made for her. Then she grew dull and miserable for want of company, and she asked leave to go home for a little while to see her father and mother, and her brothers and sisters. So the White Bear took her home again, but he told her that there was one thing she must not do; she must not go into a room with her mother alone, to talk to her, or a great misfortune would happen. When the wife of the White Bear got home, she found that her family lived in a grand house, and they were all very glad to see her; and then her mother took her into a room by themselves, and asked about her husband. And the wife of the White Bear forgot the warning, and told her mother that every night a man came and lay down with her, and went away before daylight, and that she had never seen him, and wanted to see him, very much. Then the mother said it might be a Troll she slept with; and that she ought to see what it was; and she gave her daughter a piece of candle, and said, "Light this while he is asleep, and look at him, but take care you don't drop the tallow upon him." So then the White Bear came to fetch his wife, and they went back to the palace in the hill, and that night she lit the candle, while her husband was asleep, and then she saw that he was a handsome Prince, and she felt quite in love with him, and gave him a soft kiss. But just as she kissed him she let three drops of tallow fall upon his shirt, and he woke up. Then the White Bear was very sorrowful, and said that he was enchanted by a wicked fairy, and that if his wife had only waited for a year before looking at him, the enchantment would be broken, and he would be a man again always. But now that she had given way to curiosity, he must go to a dreary castle East of the Sun and West of the Moon, and marry a witch Princess, with a nose three ells long. And then he vanished, and so did his palace, and his poor wife found herself lying in the middle of a gloomy wood, and she was dressed in rags, and was very wretched. But she did not stop to cry about her hard fate, for she was a brave girl, and made up her mind to go at once in search of her husband. So she walked for days, and then she met an old woman sitting on a hillside, and playing with a golden apple; and she asked the old woman the way to the Land East of the Sun and West of the Moon. And the old woman listened to her story, and then she said, "I don't know where it is; but you can go on and ask my next neighbour. Ride there on my horse, and when you have done with him, give him a pat under the left ear and say, 'Go home again;' and take this golden apple with you, it may be useful." So she rode on for a long way, and then came to another old woman, who was playing with a golden carding comb; and she asked her the way to the Land East of the Sun and West of the Moon? But this old woman couldn't tell her, and bade her go on to another old woman, a long way off. And she gave her the golden carding comb, and lent her a horse just like the first one. And the third old woman was playing with a golden spinning wheel; and she gave this to the wife of the White Bear, and lent her another horse, and told her to ride on to the East Wind, and ask him the way to the enchanted land. Now after a weary journey she got to the home of the East Wind, and he said he had heard of the Enchanted Prince, and of the country East of the Sun and West of the Moon, but he did not know where it was, for he had never been so far. But, he said, "Get on my back, and we will go to my brother the West Wind; perhaps he knows." So they sailed off to the West Wind, and told him the story, and he took it quite kindly, but said he didn't know the way. But perhaps his brother the South Wind might know; and they would go to him. So the White Bear's wife got on the back of the West Wind, and he blew straight away to the dwelling–place of the South Wind, and asked him where to find the Land East of the Sun and West of the Moon. But the South Wind said that although he had blown pretty nearly everywhere, he had never blown there; but he would take her to his brother the North Wind, the oldest, and strongest, and wisest Wind of all; and he would be sure to know. Now the North Wind was very cross at being disturbed, and he used bad language, and was quite rude and unpleasant. But he was a kind Wind after all, and when his brother the West Wind told him the story, he became quite fatherly, and said he would do what he could, for he knew the Land East of the Sun and West of the Moon very well. But, he said, "It is a long way off; so far off that once in my life I blew an aspen leaf there, and was so tired with it that I couldn't blow or puff for ever so many days after." So they rested that night, and next morning the North Wind puffed himself out, and got stout, and big, and strong, ready for the journey; and the maiden got upon his back, and away they went to the country East of the Sun and West of the Moon. It was a terrible journey, high up in the air, in a great storm, and over the mountains and the sea, and before they got to the end of it the North Wind grew very tired, and drooped, and nearly fell into the sea, and got so low down that the crests of the waves washed over him. But he blew as hard as he could, and at last he put the maiden down on the shore, just in front of the Enchanted Castle that stood in the Land East of the Sun and West of the Moon; and there he had to stop and rest many days before he became strong enough to blow home again.

Now the wife of the White Bear sat down before the castle, and began to play with the golden apple. And then the wicked Princess with the nose three ells long opened a window, and asked if she would sell the apple? But she said "No;" she would give the golden apple for leave to spend the night in the bed–chamber of the Prince who lived there. So the Princess with the long nose said "Yes," and the wife of the White Bear was allowed to pass the night in her husband's chamber. But a sleeping draught had been given to the Prince, and she could not wake him, though she wept greatly, and spent the whole night in crying out to him; and in the morning before he woke she was driven away by the wicked Princess. Well, next day she sat and played with the golden carding comb, and the Princess wanted that too; and the same bargain was made; but again a sleeping draught was given to the Prince, and he slept all night, and nothing could waken him; and at the first peep of daylight the wicked Princess drove the poor wife out again. Now it was the third day, and the wife of the White Bear had only the golden spinning–wheel left. So she sat and played with it, and the Princess bought it on the same terms as before. But some kind folk who slept in the next room to the Prince told him that for two nights a woman had been in his chamber, weeping bitterly, and crying out to him to wake and see her. So, being warned, the Prince only pretended to drink the sleeping draught, and so when his wife came into the room that night he was wide awake, and was rejoiced to see her; and they spent the whole night in loving talk. Now the next day was to be the Prince's wedding day; but now that his lost wife had found him, he hit upon a plan to escape marrying the Princess with the long nose. So when morning came, he said he should like to see what his bride was fit for? "Certainly," said the Witch–mother and the Princess, both together. Then the Prince said he had a fine shirt, with three drops of tallow upon it; and he would marry only the woman who could wash them out, for no other would be worth having. So they laughed at this, for they thought it would be easily done. And the Princess began, but the more she rubbed, the worse the tallow stuck to the shirt. And the old Witch—mother tried; but it got deeper and blacker than ever. And all the Trolls in the enchanted castle tried; but none of them could wash the shirt clean. Then said the Prince, "Call in the lassie who sits outside, and let her try." And she came in, and took the shirt, and washed it quite clean and white, all in a minute. Then the old Witch—mother put herself into such a rage that she burst into pieces, and so did the Princess with the long nose, and so did all the Trolls in the castle; and the Prince took his wife away with him, and all the silver and gold, and a number of Christian people who had been enchanted by the witch; and away they went for ever from the dreary Land East of the Sun and West of the Moon.

In the story of "The Soaring Lark," in the collection of German popular tales made by the brothers Grimm, we have another version of the same idea; and here, as in Eros and Psyche, and in the Land East of the Sun and West of the Moon, it is the woman to whose fault the misfortunes are laid, and upon whom falls the long and weary task of search. The story told in brief, is this. A merchant went on a journey, and promised to bring back for his three daughters whatever they wished. The eldest asked for diamonds, the second for pearls, and the youngest, who was her father's favourite, for a singing, soaring lark. As the merchant came home, he passed through a great forest, and on the top bough of a tall tree he found a lark, and tried to take it. Then a Lion sprang from behind the tree, and said the lark was his, and that he would eat up the merchant for trying to steal it. The merchant told the Lion why he wanted the bird, and then the Lion said that he would give him the lark, and let him go, on one condition, namely, that he should give to the Lion the first thing or person that met him on his return. Now the first person who met the merchant when he got home was his youngest daughter, and the poor merchant told her the story, and wept very much, and said that she should not go into the forest. But the daughter said, "What you have promised you must do;" and so she went into the forest, to find the Lion. The Lion was an Enchanted Prince, and all his servants were also turned into lions; and so they remained all day; but at night they all changed back again into men. Now when the Lion Prince saw the merchant's daughter, he fell in love with her, and took her to a fine castle, and at night, when he became a man, they were married, and lived very happily, and in great splendour. One day the Prince said to his wife, "To—morrow your eldest sister is to be married; if you would like to be there, my lions shall go with you." So she went, and the lions with her, and there were great rejoicings in her father's house, because they were afraid that she had been torn to pieces in the forest; and after staying some time, she went back to her husband. After a while, the Prince said to his wife, "To-morrow your second sister is going to be married," and she replied, "This time I will not go alone, for you shall go with me." Then he told her how dangerous that would be, for if a single ray from a burning light fell upon him, he would be changed into a Dove, and in that form would have to fly about for seven years. But the Princess very much wanted him to go, and in order to protect him from the light, she had a room built with thick walls, so that no light could get through, and there he was to sit while the bridal candles were burning. But by some accident, the door of the room was made of new wood, which split, and made a little chink, and through this chink one ray of light from the torches of the bridal procession fell like a hair upon the Prince, and he was instantly changed in form; and when his wife came to tell him that all danger was over, she found only a White Dove, who said very sadly to her—

"For seven years I must fly about in the world, but at every seventh mile I will let fall a white feather and a drop of red blood, which will show you the way, and if you follow it, you may save me."

Then the White Dove flew out of the door, and the Princess followed it, and at every seventh mile the Dove let fall a white feather and a drop of red blood; and so, guided by the feathers and the drops of blood, she followed the Dove, until the seven years had almost passed, and she began to hope that the Prince's enchantment would be at an end. But one day there was no white feather to be seen, nor any drop of red blood, and the Dove had flown quite away. Then the poor Princess thought, "No man can help me now;" and so she mounted up to the Sun, and said, "Thou shinest into every chasm and over every peak; hast thou seen a White Dove on the wing?"

"No," answered the Sun. "I have not seen one; but take this casket, and open it when you are in need of help."

She took the casket, and thanked the Sun. When evening came, she asked the Moon—

"Hast thou seen a White Dove? for thou shinest all night long over every field and through every wood."

"No," said the Moon, "I have not seen a White Dove; but here is an egg—break it when you are in great trouble."

She thanked the Moon, and took the egg; and then the North Wind came by; and she said to the North Wind:

"Hast thou not seen a White Dove? for thou passest through all the boughs, and shakest every leaf under heaven."

"No," said the North Wind, "I have not seen one; but I will ask my brothers, the East Wind, and the West Wind, and the South Wind."

So he asked them all three; and the East Wind and the West Wind said, "No, they had not seen the White Dove;" but the South Wind said—

"I have seen the White Dove; he has flown to the Red Sea, and has again been changed into a Lion, for the seven years are up; and the Lion stands there in combat with an Enchanted Princess, who is in the form of a great Caterpillar."

Then the North Wind knew what to do; and he said to the Princess—

"Go to the Red Sea; on the right–hand shore there are great reeds, count them, and cut off the eleventh reed, and beat the Caterpillar with it. Then the Caterpillar and the Lion will take their human forms. Then look for the Griffin which sits on the Red Sea, and leap upon its back with the Prince, and the Griffin will carry you safely home. Here is a nut; let it fall when you are in the midst of the sea, and a large nut–tree will grow out of the water, and the Griffin will rest upon it."

So the Princess went to the Red Sea, and counted the reeds, and cut off the eleventh reed, and beat the Caterpillar with it, and then the Lion conquered in the fight, and both of them took their human forms again. But the Enchanted Princess was too quick for the poor wife, for she instantly seized the Prince and sprang upon the back of the Griffin, and away they flew, quite out of sight. Now the poor deserted wife sat down on the desolate shore, and cried bitterly; and then she said, "So far as the wind blows, and so long as the cock crows, will I search for my husband, till I find him;" and so she travelled on and on, until one day she came to the palace whither the Enchanted Princess had carried the

Prince; and there was great feasting going on, and they told her that the Prince and Princess were about to be married. Then she remembered what the Sun had said, and took out the casket and opened it, and there was the most beautiful dress in all the world; as brilliant as the Sun himself. So she put it on, and went into the palace, and everybody admired the dress, and the Enchanted Princess asked if she would sell it?

"Not for gold or silver," she said, "but for flesh and blood."

"What do you mean?" the Princess asked.

"Let me sleep for one night in the bridegroom's chamber," the wife said. So the Enchanted Princess agreed, but she gave the Prince a sleeping draught, so that he could not hear his wife's cries; and in the morning she was driven out, without a word from him, for he slept so soundly that all she said seemed to him only like the rushing of the wind through the fir–trees.

Then the poor wife sat down and wept again, until she thought of the egg the Moon had given her; and when she took the egg and broke it, there came out of it a hen with twelve chickens, all of gold, and the chickens pecked quite prettily, and then ran under the wings of the hen for shelter. Presently, the Enchanted Princess looked out of the window, and saw the hen and the chickens, and asked if they were for sale. "Not for gold or silver, but for flesh and blood," was the answer she got; and then the wife made the same bargain as before—that she should spend the night in the bridegroom's chamber. Now this night the Prince was warned by his servant, and so he poured away the sleeping draught instead of drinking it; and when his wife came, and told her sorrowful story, he knew her, and said, "Now I am saved;" and then they both went as quickly as possible, and set themselves upon the Griffin, who carried them over the Red Sea; and when they got to the middle of the sea, the Princess let fall the nut which the North Wind had given to her, and a great nut–tree grew up at once, on which the Griffin rested; and then it went straight to their home, where they lived happy ever after.

One more story of the same kind must be told, for three reasons: because it is very good reading, because it brings together various legends, and because it shows that these were common to Celtic as well as to Hindu, Greek, Teutonic, and Scandinavian peoples. It is called "The Battle of the Birds," and is given at full length, and in several different versions, in Campbell's "Popular Tales of the West Highlands."[5] To bring it within our space we must tell it in our own way.

Once upon a time every bird and other creature gathered to battle. The son of the King of Tethertoun went to see the battle, but it was over before he got there, all but one fight, between a great Raven and a Snake; and the Snake was getting the victory. The King's son helped the Raven, and cut off the Snake's head. The Raven thanked him for his kindness and said, "Now I will give thee a sight; come up on my wings;" and then the Raven flew with him over seven mountains, and seven glens, and seven moors, and that night the King's son lodged in the house of the Raven's sisters; and promised to meet the Raven next morning in the same place. This went on for three nights and days, and on the third morning, instead of a raven, there met him a handsome lad, who gave him a bundle, and told him not to look into it, until he was in the place where he would most wish to dwell. But the King's son did look into the bundle, and then he found himself in a great castle with fine grounds about it, and he was very sorry, because he wished the castle had been near his father's house, but he could not put it back into the bundle again. Then a great Giant met him, and offered to put the castle back into a bundle for a reward, and this was to be the Prince's son, when the son was seven years old. So the Prince promised, and the Giant put everything back into the bundle, and the Prince went home with it to his father's house. When he got there he opened the bundle, and out came the castle and all the rest, just as before, and at the castle door stood a beautiful maiden who asked him to marry her, and they were married, and had a son. When the seven years were up, the Giant came to ask for the boy, and then the King's son (who had now become a king himself) told his wife about his promise. "Leave that to me and the Giant," said the Queen. So she dressed the cook's son (who was the right age) in fine clothes, and gave him to the Giant; but the Giant gave the boy a rod, and asked him, "If thy father had that rod, what would he do with it?" "He would beat the dogs if they went near the King's meat," said the boy. Then Said the Giant, "Thou art the cook's son," and he killed him. Then the Giant went back, very angry, and the Queen gave him the butler's son; and the Giant gave him the rod, and asked him the same question, "My father would beat the dogs if they came near the King's glasses," said the boy. "Thou art the butler's son," said the Giant; and he killed him. Now the Giant went back the third time, and made a dreadful noise. "Out here *thy* son," he said, "or the stone that is highest in thy dwelling shall be the lowest." So they gave him the King's son, and the Giant took him to his own house, and he stayed there a long while. One day the youth heard sweet music at the top of the Giant's house, and he saw a sweet face. It was the Giant's youngest daughter; and she said to him, "My father wants you to marry one of my sisters, and he wants me to marry the King of the Green City, but I will not. So when he asks, say thou wilt take me." Next day the Giant gave the King's son choice of his two eldest daughters; but the Prince said, "Give me this pretty little one?" and then the Giant was angry, and said that before he had her he must do three things. The first of these was to clean out a byre or cattle place, where there was the dung of a hundred cattle, and it had not been cleaned for seven years. He tried to do it, and worked till noon, but the filth was as bad as ever. Then the Giant's youngest daughter came, and bid him sleep, and she cleaned out the stable, so that a golden apple would run from end to end of it. Next day the Giant set him to thatch the byre with birds' down, and he had to go out on the moors to catch the birds; but at midday, he had caught only two blackbirds, and then the Giant's youngest daughter came again, and bid him sleep, and then she caught the birds, and thatched the byre with the feathers before sundown. The third day the Giant set him another task. In the forest there was a fir–tree, and at the top was a magpie's nest, and in the nest were five eggs, and he was to bring these five eggs to the Giant without breaking one of them. Now the tree was very tall; from the ground to the first branch it was five hundred feet, so that the King's son could not climb up it. Then the Giant's youngest daughter came again, and she put her fingers one after the other into the tree, and made a ladder for the King's son to climb up by. When he was at the nest at the very top, she said, "Make haste now with the eggs, for my father's breath is burning my back;" and she was in such a hurry that she left her little finger sticking in the top of the tree. Then she told the King's son that the Giant would make all his daughters look alike, and dress them alike, and that when the choosing time came he was to look at their hands, and take the one that had not a little finger on one hand. So it happened, and the King's son chose the youngest daughter, because she put out her hand to guide him.

Then they were married, and there was a great feast, and they went to their chamber. The Giant's daughter said to her husband, "Sleep not, or thou diest; we must fly quick, or my father will kill thee." So first she cut an apple into nine pieces, and put two pieces at the head of the bed, and two at the foot, and two at the door of the kitchen, and two at the great door, and one outside the house. And then she and her husband went to the stable, and mounted the fine grey filly, and rode off as fast as they could. Presently the Giant called out, "Are you asleep yet?" and the apple at the head of the bed said, "We are not asleep." Then he called again, and the apple at the foot of the bed said the same thing; and then he asked again and again, until the apple outside the house door answered; and then he knew that a trick had been played on him, and ran to the bedroom and found it empty. And then he pursued the runaways as fast as possible. Now at day–break—"at the mouth of day," the story- teller says—the Giant's daughter said to her husband, "My father's breath is burning my back; put thy hand into the ear of the grey filly, and whatever thou findest, throw it behind thee." "There is a twig of sloe–tree," he said. "Throw it behind thee," said she; and he did so, and twenty miles of black–thorn wood grew out of it, so thick that a weasel could not get through. But the Giant cut through it with his big axe and his wood–knife, and went after them again. At the heat of day the Giant's daughter said again, "My father's breath is burning my back;" and then her husband put his finger in the filly's ear, and took out a piece of grey stone, and threw it behind him, and there grew up directly a great rock twenty miles broad and twenty miles high. Then the Giant got his mattock and his lever, and made a way through the rocks, and came after them again. Now it was near sunset, and once more the Giant's daughter felt her father's breath burning her back. So, for the third time, her husband put his hand into the filly's ear, and took out a bladder of water, and he threw it behind him, and there was a fresh–water loch, twenty miles long and twenty miles broad; and the Giant came on so fast that he ran into the middle of the loch and was drowned.

Here is clearly a Sun–myth, which is like those of ancient Hindu and Greek legend: the blue–grey Filly is the Dawn, on which the new day, the maiden and her lover, speed away. The great Giant, whose breath burns the maiden's back, is the morning Sun, whose progress is stopped by the thick shade of the trees. Then he rises higher, and at midday he breaks through the forest, and soars above the rocky mountains. At evening, still powerful in speed and heat, he comes to the great lake, plunges into it, and sets, and those whom he pursues escape. This ending is repeated in one of the oldest Hindu mythical stories, that of Bheki, the Frog Princess, who lives with her husband on condition that he never shows her a drop of water. One day he forgets, and she disappears: that is, the sun sets or dies on the water—a fanciful idea which takes us straight as an arrow to Aryan myths.

Now, however, we must complete the Gaelic story, which here becomes like the Soaring Lark, and the Land East of the Sun and West of the Moon, and other Teutonic and Scandinavian tales.

After the Giant's daughter and her husband had got free from the Giant, she bade him go to his father's house, and tell them about her; but he was not to suffer anything to kiss him, or he would forget her altogether. So he told everybody they were not to kiss him, but an old greyhound leapt up at him, and touched his mouth, and then he forgot all about the Giant's daughter, just as if she had never lived. Now when the King's son left her, the poor forgotten wife sat beside a well, and when night came she climbed into an oak–tree, and slept amongst the branches. There was a shoemaker who lived near the well, and next day he sent his wife to fetch water, and as she drew it she saw what she fancied to be her own reflection in the water, but it was really the likeness of the maiden in the tree above it. The shoemaker's wife, however, thinking it was her own, imagined herself to be very handsome, and so she went back and told the shoemaker that she was too beautiful to be his thrall, or slave, any longer, and so she went off. The same thing happened to the shoemaker's daughter; and she went off too. Then the man himself went to the well, and saw the maiden in the tree, and understood it all, and asked her to come down and stay at his house, and to be his daughter. So she went with him. After a while there came three gentlemen from the King's Court, and each of them wanted to marry her; and she agreed with each of them privately, on condition that each should give a sum of money for a wedding gift. Well, they agreed to this, each unknown to the other; and she married one of them, but when he came and had paid the money, she gave him a cup of water to hold, and there he had to stand, all night long, unable to move or to let go the cup of water, and in the morning he went away ashamed, but said nothing to his friends. Next night it was the turn of the second; and she told him to see that the door–latch was fastened; and when he touched the latch he could not let it go, and had to stand there all night holding it; and so he went away, and said nothing. The next night the third came, and when he stepped upon the floor, one foot stuck so fast that he could not draw it out until morning; and then he did the same as the others—went off quite cast down. And then the maiden gave all the money to the shoemaker for his kindness to her. This is like the story of "The Master Maid," in Dr. Dasent's collection of "Tales from the Norse." But there is the end of it to come. The shoemaker had to finish some shoes because the young King was going to be married; and the maiden said she should like to see the King before he married. So the shoemaker took her to the King's castle; and then she went into the wedding–room, and because of her beauty they filled a vessel of wine for her. When she was going to drink it, there came a flame out of the glass, and out of the flame there came a silver pigeon and a golden pigeon; and just then three grains of barley fell upon the floor, and the silver pigeon ate them up. Then the golden one said, "If thou hadst mind when I cleaned the byre, thou wouldst not eat that without giving me a share." Then three more grains fell, and the silver pigeon ate them also. Then said the golden pigeon, "If thou hadst mind when I thatched the byre, thou wouldst not eat that without giving me a share." Then three other grains fell, and the silver pigeon ate them up. And the golden pigeon said, "If thou hadst mind when I harried the magpie's nest, thou wouldst not eat that without giving me my share. I lost my little finger bringing it down, and I want it still." Then, suddenly, the King's son remembered, and knew who it was, and sprang to her and kissed her from hand to mouth; and the priest came, and they were married.

These stories will be enough to show how the same idea repeats itself in different ways among various peoples who have come from the same stock: for the ancient Hindu legend of Urvasi and Pururavas, the Greek fable of Eros and Psyche, the Norse story of the Land East of the Sun and West of the Moon, the Teutonic story of the Soaring Lark, and the Celtic story of the Battle of the Birds, are all one and the same in their general character, their origin, and their meaning; and in all these respects they resemble the story which we know so well in English—that of Beauty and the Beast. The same kind of likeness has already been shown in the story of Cinderella, and in those which resemble it in the older Aryan legends and in the later stories of the Greeks. If space allowed, such comparisons might be carried much further; indeed, there is no famous fairy tale known to children in our day which has not proceeded from our Aryan forefathers, thousands of years ago, and which is not repeated in Hindu, Persian, Greek, Teutonic, Scandinavian, and Celtic folk–lore; the stories being always the same in their leading idea, and yet always so different in their details as to show that the story–tellers have not copied from each other, but that they are repeating, in their own way, legends and fancies which existed thousands of years ago, before the Aryan people broke up from their old homes, and went southward and westward, and spread themselves over India and throughout Europe.

Now there is a curious little German story, called "The Wolf and the Seven Little Kids," which is told in Grimm's collection, and which shows at once the connection between Teutonic folk–lore, and Greek mythology, and Aryan legend. There was an old Goat who had seven young ones, and when she went into the forest for wood, she warned them against the Wolf; if he came, they were not to open the door to him on any account. Presently the Wolf came, and knocked, and asked to be let in; but the little Kids said, "No, you have a gruff voice; you are a wolf." So the Wolf went and bought a large piece of chalk, and ate it up, and by this means he made his voice smooth; and then he came back to the cottage, and knocked, and again asked to be let in. The little Kids, however, saw his black paws, and they said, "No, your feet are black; you are a wolf." Then the Wolf went to a baker, and got him to powder his feet with flour; and when the little Kids saw his white feet, they thought it was their mother, and let him in. Then the little Kids were very much frightened, and ran and hid themselves. The first got under the table, the second into the bed, the third into the cupboard, the fourth into the kitchen, the fifth into the oven, the sixth into the wash-tub, and the seventh into the clock-case. The wicked Wolf, however, found all of them out, and ate them up, excepting the one in the clock-case, where he did not think of looking. And when the greedy monster had finished his meal, he went into the meadow, and lay down and slept. Just at this time the old Goat came home, and began crying for her children; but the only one who answered was the youngest, who said, "Here I am, dear mother, in the clock-case;" and then he came out and told her all about it. Presently the Goat went out into the meadow, and there lay the Wolf, snoring quite loud; and she thought she saw something stirring in his body. So she ran back, and fetched a pair of scissors and a needle and thread, and then she cut open the monster's hairy coat, and out jumped first one little kid, and then another, until all the six stood round her, for the greedy Wolf was in such a hurry that he had swallowed them whole. Then the Goat and the little Kids brought a number of stones, and put them into the Wolf's stomach, and sewed up the place again. When the Wolf woke up, he felt very thirsty, and ran off to the brook to drink, and the heavy stones overbalanced him, so that he fell into the brook, and was drowned. And then the seven little Kids danced round their mother, singing joyfully, "The wolf is dead! the wolf is dead!" Now this story is nothing but another version of an old Greek legend which tells how Kronos (Time), an ancient god, devoured his children while they were quite young; and Kronos was the son of Ouranos, which means the heavens; and Ouranos is a name which comes from that of Varuna, a god of the sky in the old sacred books, or Vedas, of the Hindus; and the meaning of the legend is that Night swallows up or devours the days of the week, all but the youngest, which still exists, because, like the little kid in the German tale, it is in the clock-case.

Again, in the Vedas we have many accounts of the fights of Indra, the sun-god, with dragons and monsters, which mean the dark-clouds, the tempest thunder-bearing clouds, which were supposed to have stolen the heavenly cows, or the light, pleasant, rain-bearing clouds, and to have shut them up in gloomy caverns. From this source we have an infinite number of Greek and Teutonic, and Scandinavian, and other legends. One of these is the story of Polyphemos, the great one-eyed giant, or Kyklops, whom Odysseus blinded. Polyphemos is the storm-cloud, and Odysseus stands for the sun. The storm-cloud threatens the mariners; the lightnings dart from the spot which seems like an eye in the darkness; he hides the blue heavens and the soft white clouds—the cows of the sky, or the white-fleeced flocks of heaven. Then comes Odysseus, the sun-god, the hero, and smites him blind, and chases him away, and disperses the threatening and the danger, and brings light, and peace, and calm again.

Now this legend of Polyphemos is to be found everywhere; in the oldest Hindu books, in Teutonic, and Norse, and Slav stories; and everywhere also the great giant, stormy, angry, and one–eyed, is always very stupid, and is always overthrown or outwitted by the hero, Odysseus, when he is shut up in the cavern of Polyphemos, cheats the monster by tying himself under the belly of the largest and oldest ram, and so passes out while the blind giant feels the fleece, and thinks that all is safe. Almost exactly the same trick is told in an old Gaelic story, that of Conall Cra Bhuidhe.[6] A great Giant with only one eye seized upon Conall, who was hunting on the Giant's lands. Conall himself is made to tell the story:

"I hear a great clattering coming, and what was there but a great Giant and his dozen of goats with him, and a buck at their head. And when the Giant had tied the goats, he came up, and he said to me, 'Hao O! Conall, it's long since my knife is rusting in my pouch waiting for thy tender flesh.' 'Och!' said I, 'it's not much thou wilt be bettered by me, though thou shouldst tear me asunder; I will make but one meal for thee. But I see that thou art one–eyed. I am a good leech, and I will give thee the sight of the other eye.' The Giant went and he drew the great caldron on the site of the fire. I was telling him how he should heat the water, so that I should give its sight to the other eye. I got leather and I made a rubber of it, and I set him upright in the caldron. I began at the eye that was well, till I left them as bad as each other. When he saw that he could not see a glimpse, and when I myself said to him that I would get out in spite of him, he gave that spring out of the water, and he stood in the mouth of the cave, and he said that he would have revenge for the sight of his eye. I had but to stay there crouched the length of the night, holding in my breath in such a way that he might not feel where I was. When he felt the birds calling in the morning, and knew that the day was, he said, 'Art thou sleeping? Awake, and let out my lot of goats!' I killed the buck. He cried, 'I will not believe that thou art not killing my buck.' 'I am not,' I said, 'but the ropes are so tight that I take long to loose them.' I let out one of the goats, and he was caressing her, and he said to her, 'There thou art, thou shaggy hairy white goat; and thou seest me, but I see thee not.' I was letting them out, by way of one by one, as I flayed the buck, and before the last one was out I had him flayed, bag–wise. Then I went and put my legs in the place of his legs, and my hands in the place of his fore–legs, and my head in the place of his head, and the horns on top of my head, so that the brute might think it was the buck. I went out. When I was going out the Giant laid his hand on me, and said, 'There thou art, thou pretty buck; thou seest me, but I see

37

thee not.' When I myself got out, and I saw the world about me, surely joy was on me. When I was out and had shaken the skin off me, I said to the brute, 'I am out now, in spite of thee!'"

It was a blind fiddler, in Islay, who told the story of Conall, as it had been handed down by tradition from generation to generation; just as thousands of years before the story of Odysseus and Polyphemos was told by Greek bards to wondering villagers.

Here we must stop; for volumes would not contain all that might be said of the likeness of legend to legend in all the branches of the Aryan family, or of the meaning of these stories, and of the lessons they teach—lessons of history, and religious belief, and customs, and morals and ways of thought, and poetic fancies, and of well−nigh all things, heavenly and human— stretching back to the very spring and cradle of our race, older than the oldest writings, and yet so ever fresh and new that while great scholars ponder over them for their deep meaning, little children in the nursery or by the fire−side in winter listen to them with delight for their wonder and their beauty. Else, if there were time and space we might tell the story of Jason, and show how it springs from the changes of day and night, and how the hero, in his good ship Argo, our mother Earth, searches for and bears away in triumph the Golden Fleece, the beams of the radiant sun. Or we might fly with Perseus on his weary, endless journey—the light pursuing and scattering the darkness; the glittering hero, borne by the mystic sandals of Hermes, bearing the sword of the sunlight, piercing the twilight or gloaming in the land of the mystic Graiae; slaying Medusa, the solemn star−lit night; destroying the dark dragon, and setting free Andromeda the dawn−maiden; and doing many wonders more. Or in Hermes we might trace out the Master Thief of Teutonic, and Scandinavian, and Hindu legends; or in Herakles, the type of the heroes who are god−like in their strength, yet who do the bidding of others, and who suffer toil and wrong, and die glorious deaths, and leave great names for men to wonder at: heroes such as Odysseus, and Theseus, and Phoebus, and Achilles, and Sigurd, and Arthur, and all of whom represent, in one form or another, the great mystery of Nature, and the conflict of light and darkness; and so, if we look to their deeper meaning, the constant triumph of good over evil, and of right over wrong.

---

[3] *Oxford Essays:* "Comparative Mythology," p. 69.

[4] *Popular Tales from the Norse*, by George Webbe Dasent, D.C.L.

[5] *Popular Titles of the West Highlands*. Orally collected,
with a Translation by J. F. Campbell. Edinburgh: Edmonton
and Douglas. 4 vols.

[6] Campbell's *Popular Tales of the West Highlands*, i. 112.

CHAPTER III. DWELLERS IN FAIRYLAND: STORIES FROM THE EAST.

We have said something about the people and the countries which gave birth to our Fairy
Stories, and about the meaning of such tales generally when they were first thought of.
Then they were clearly understood, and those who told them and heard them knew what
they meant; but, as time went on, and as the Aryan race became scattered in various
countries, the old stories changed a great deal, and their meaning was lost, and all kinds
of wild legends, and strange fables and fanciful tales, were made out of them. The earliest
stories were about clouds, and winds, and the sun, and the waters, and the earth, which
were turned into Gods and other beings of a heavenly kind. By degrees, as the first
meanings of the legends were lost, these beings gave place to a multitude of others: some
of them beautiful, and good, and kind and friendly to mankind; and some of them terrible,
and bad, and malignant, and always trying to do harm; and there were so many of both
kinds that all the world was supposed to be full of them. There were Spirits of the water,
and the air, and the earth, forest and mountain demons, creatures who dwelt in darkness
and in fire, and others who lived in the sunshine, or loved to come out only in the
moonlight. There were some, again—Dwarfs, and other creatures of that kind—who
made their homes in caves and underground places, and heaped up treasures of gold and
silver, and gems, and made wonderful works in metals of all descriptions; and there were
giants, some of them with two heads, who could lift mountains, and walk through rivers
and seas, and who picked up great rocks and threw them about like pebbles. Then there
were Ogres, with shining rows of terrible teeth, who caught up men and women and
children, and strung them together like larks, and carried them home, and cooked them
for supper. Then, also, there were Good Spirits, of the kind the Arabs call Peris, and we
call Fairies, who made it their business to defend deserving people against the wicked
monsters; and there were Magicians, and other wise or cunning people, who had power
over the spirits, whether good or bad, as you read in the story of Aladdin and his Ring,
and his Wonderful Lamp, and in other tales in the "Arabian Nights," and collections of

that kind. Many of these beings—all of whom, for our purpose, may be called Dwellers in Fairyland—had the power of taking any shape they pleased, like the Ogre in the story of "Puss in Boots," who changed himself first into a lion, and then into an elephant, and then into a mouse, when he got eaten up; and they could also change human beings into different forms, or turn them into stone, or carry them about in the air from place to place, and put them under the spells of enchantment, as they liked.

Some of the most wonderful creatures of Fairyland are to be found in Eastern stories, the tales of India, and Arabia, and Persia. Here we have the Divs, and Jinns, and Peris, and Rakshas—who were the originals of our own Ogres—and terrible giants, and strange mis–shapen dwarfs, and vampires and monsters of various kinds. Many others, also very wonderful, are to be found in what is called the Mythology—that is, the fables and stories—of ancient Greece, such as the giant Atlas, who bore the world upon his shoulders; and Polyphemus, the one–eyed giant, who caught Odysseus and his companions, and shut them up in his cave; and Kirke, the beautiful sorceress, who turned men into swine; and the Centaurs, creatures half men and half horses; and the Gorgon Medusa, whose head, with its hair of serpents, turned into stone all who beheld it; and the great dragon, the Python, whom Phoebus killed, and who resembles the dragon Vritra, in Hindu legend—the dragon slain by Indra, the god of the Sun, because he shut up the rain, and so scorched the earth—and who also resembles Fafnir, the dragon of Scandinavian legend, killed by Sigurd; and the fabled dragon with whom St. George fought; and also, the dragon of Wantley, whom our old English legends describe as being killed by More of More Hall. In the stories of the North lands of Europe, as we are told in the Eddas and Sagas (the songs and records), there are likewise many wonderful beings—the Trolls, the Frost Giants, curious dwarfs, elves, nisses, mermen and mermaids, and swan–maidens and the like. The folk–lore—that is, the common traditionary stories—of Germany are full of such wonders. Here, again, we have giants and dwarfs and kobolds; and birds and beasts and fishes who can talk; and good fairies, who come in and help their friends just when they are wanted; and evil fairies, and witches; and the wild huntsman, who sweeps across the sky with his ghostly train; and men and women who turn themselves into wolves, and go about in the night devouring sheep and killing human beings, In Russian tales we find many creatures of the same kind, and also in those of Italy, and Spain, and France. And in our own islands we have them too, for the traditions of English giants, and ogres, and dwarfs still linger in the tales of Jack the Giant–killer and Jack and the Bean–stalk, and Hop o' my Thumb; and we have also the elves whom Shakspeare draws for us so delightfully in "Midsummer Night's Dream" and in "The Merry Wives of

Windsor"; and there are the Devonshire pixies; and the Scottish fairies and the brownies—the spirits who do the work of the house or the farm—and the Irish "good people;" and the Pooka, which comes in the form of a wild colt; and the Leprechaun, a dwarf who makes himself look like a little old man, mending shoes; and the Banshee, which cries and moans when great people are going to die.

To all these, and more, whom there is no room to mention, we must add other dwellers in Fairyland—forms, in one shape or other, of the great Sun–myths of the ancient Aryan race—such as Arthur and the Knights of the Round Table and Vivien and Merlin, and Queen Morgan le hay, and Ogier the Dane, and the story of Roland, and the Great Norse poems which tell of Sigurd, and Brynhilt, and Gudrun, and the Niblung folk. And to these, again, there are to be added many of the heroes and heroines who figure in the Thousand–and–one Nights—such, for example, as Aladdin, and Sindbad, and Ali Baba, and the Forty Thieves, and the Enchanted Horse, and the Fairy Peri Banou, with her wonderful tent that would cover an army, and her brother Schaibar, the dwarf, with his beard thirty feet long, and his great bar of iron with which he could sweep down a city. Even yet we have not got to the end of the long list of Fairy Folk, for there are still to be reckoned the well–known characters who figure in our modern Fairy Tales, such as Cinderella, and the Yellow Dwarf, and the White Cat, and Fortunatus, and Beauty and the Beast, and Riquet with the Tuft, and the Invisible Prince, and many more whom children know by heart, and whom all of us, however old we may be, still cherish with fond remembrance, because they give us glimpses into the beautiful and wondrous land, the true Fairyland whither good King Arthur went—

> "The island–valley of Avilion,
> Where falls not hail, or rain, or any snow,
> Nor ever wind blows loudly; but it lies
> Deep–meadowed, happy, fair with orchard lawns,
> And bowery hollows crowned with summer sea."

Now it is plain that we cannot speak of all these dwellers in Fairyland; but we can only pick out a few here and there, and those of you who want to know more must go to the books that tell of them. As to me, who have undertaken to tell something of these wonders, I feel very much like the poor boy in the little German story of "The Golden Key." Do you know the story? If you don't, I will tell it you. "One winter, when a deep snow was lying on the ground, a poor boy had to go out in a sledge to fetch wood. When he had got enough he thought he would make a fire to warm himself, for his limbs were quite frozen. So he swept the snow away and made a clear space, and there he found a golden key. Then he began to think that where there was a key there must also be a lock; and digging in the earth he found a small iron chest. 'I hope the key will fit,' lie said to himself, 'for there must certainly be great treasures in this box.' After looking all round the box he found a little keyhole, and to his great joy, the golden key fitted it exactly. Then he turned the key once round"—and now we must wait till he has quite unlocked it and lifted the lid up, and then we shall learn what wonderful treasures were in the chest. This is all that this book can do for you. It can give you the golden key, and show you where the chest is to be found, and then you must unlock it for yourselves.

Where shall we begin our hasty journey into Wonderland? Suppose we take a glance at those famous Hindu demons, the Rakshas, who are the originals of all the ogres and giants of our nursery tales? Now the Rakshas were very terrible creatures indeed, and in the minds of many people in India are so still, for they are believed in even now. Their natural form, so the stories say, is that of huge, unshapely giants, like clouds, with hair and beard of the colour of the red lightning; but they can take any form they please, to deceive those whom they wish to devour, for their great delight, like that of the ogres, is to kill all they meet, and to eat the flesh of those whom they kill. Often they appear as hunters, of monstrous size, with tusks instead of teeth, and with horns on their heads, and all kinds of grotesque and frightful weapons and ornaments. They are very strong, and make themselves stronger by various arts of magic; and they are strongest of all at nightfall, when they are supposed to roam about the jungles, to enter the tombs, and even to make their way into the cities, and carry off their victims. But the Rakshas are not alone like ogres in their cruelty, but also in their fondness for money, and for precious stones, which they get together in great quantities and conceal in their palaces; for some of them are kings of their species, and have thousands upon thousands of inferior Rakshas under their command. But while they are so numerous and so powerful, the Rakshas, like all the ogres and giants in Fairyland, are also very stupid, and are easily outwitted by clever people. There are many Hindu stories which are told to show this. I will tell you one of them.[7] Two little Princesses were badly treated at home, and so they ran away into a great forest, where they found a palace belonging to a Rakshas, who had gone out. So they went into the house and feasted, and swept the rooms, and made everything neat and tidy. Just as they had done this, the Rakshas and his wife came home, and the two Princesses ran up to the top of the house, and hid themselves on the flat roof. When the Rakshas got indoors he said to his wife: "Somebody has been making everything clean and tidy. Wife, did you do this?" "No," she said; "I don't know who can have done it." "Some one has been sweeping the court–yard," said the Rakshas. "Wife, did you sweep the court–yard?" "No," she answered; "I did not do it." Then the Rakshas walked round and round several times, with his nose up in the air, saying, "Some one is here now; I smell flesh and blood. Where can they be?" "Stuff and nonsense!" cried the Rakshas' wife. "You smell flesh and blood, indeed! Why, you have just been killing and eating a hundred thousand people. I should wonder if you didn't still smell flesh and blood!" They went on disputing, till at last the Rakshas gave it up. "Never mind," lie said; "I don't know how it is—I am very thirsty: let's come and drink some water." So they went to the well, and began letting down jars into it, and drawing them up, and drinking the water. Then the elder of the two Princesses, who was very bold and wise, said to her sister, "I will do something that will be very good for us both." So she ran quickly down stairs, and crept close behind the Rakshas and his wife, as they stood on tip–toe more than half over the side of the well, and catching hold of one of the Rakshas' heels, and one of his wife's, she gave each a little push, and down they both tumbled into the well, and were drowned—the Rakshas and the Rakshas' wife. The Princess then went back to her sister, and said, "I have killed the Rakshas!" "What, both?" cried her sister. "Yes, both," she said. "Won't they come back?" said her sister. "No, never," answered she.

This, you see, is something like the story of the Little Girl and the Three Bears, so well known amongst our Nursery Tales.

Another story will show you how stupid a Rakshas is, and how easily he can be outwitted.[8]

Once upon a time a Blind Man and a Deaf Man made an agreement. The Blind Man was to hear for the Deaf Man; and the Deaf Man was to see for the Blind Man; and so they were to go about on their travels together. One day they went to a nautch—that is, a singing and dancing exhibition. The Deaf Man said, "The dancing is very good; but the music is not worth listening to." "I do not agree with you," the Blind Man said; "I think the music is very good; but the dancing is not worth looking at." So they went away for a walk in the jungle. On the way they found a donkey, belonging to a dhobee, or washerman, and a big chattee, or iron pot, which the washerman used to boil clothes in. "Brother," said the Deaf Man, "here is a donkey and a chattee; let us take them with us, they may be useful." So they took them, and went on. Presently they came to an ants'

43

nest. "Here," said the Deaf Man, "are a number of very fine black ants; let us take some of them to show our friends." "Yes," said the Blind Man, "they will do as presents to our friends." So the Deaf Man took out a silver box from his pocket, and put several of the black ants into it. After a time a terrible storm came on. "Oh dear!" cried the Deaf Man, "how dreadful this lightning is! let us get to some place of shelter." "I don't see that it's dreadful at all," said the Blind Man, "but the thunder is terrible; let us get under shelter." So they went up to a building that looked like a temple, and went in, and took the donkey and the big pot and the black ants with them. But it was not a temple, it was the house of a powerful Rakshas, and the Rakshas came home as soon as they had got inside and had fastened the door. Finding that he couldn't get in, he began to make a great noise, louder than the thunder, and he beat upon the door with his great fists. Now the Deaf Man looked through a chink, and saw him, and was very frightened, for the Rakshas was dreadful to look at. But the Blind Man, as he couldn't see, was very brave; and he went to the door and called out, "Who are you? and what do you mean by coming here and battering at the door in this way, and at this time of night?" "I'm a Rakshas," he answered, in a rage; "and this is my house, and if you don't let me in I will kill you." Then the Blind Man called out in reply, "Oh! you're a Rakshas, are you? Well, if you're Rakshas, I'm Bakshas, and Bakshas is as good as Rakshas." "What nonsense is this?" cried the monster; "there is no such creature as a Bakshas." "Go away," replied the Blind Man, "if you make any further disturbance I'll punish you; for know that I *am* Bakshas, and Bakshas is Rakshas' father." "Heavens and earth!" cried the Rakshas, "I never heard such an extraordinary thing in my life. But if you are my father, let me see your face,"—for he began to get puzzled and frightened, as the person inside was so very positive. Now the Blind Man and the Deaf Man didn't quite know what to do; but at last they opened the door just a little, and poked the donkey's nose out. "Bless me," thought the Rakshas, "what a terribly ugly face my father Bakshas has got." Then he called out again "O! father Bakshas, you have a very big fierce face, but people have sometimes very big heads and very little bodies; let me see you, body and head, before I go away." Then the Blind Man and the Deaf Man rolled the great iron pot across the floor with a thundering noise; and the Rakshas, who watched the chink of the door very carefully, said to himself, "He has got a great body as well, so I had better go away." But he was still doubtful; so he said, "Before I go away let me hear you scream," for all the tribe of the Rakshas scream dreadfully. Then the Blind Man and the Deaf Man took two of the black ants out of the box, and put one into each of the donkey's ears, and the ants bit the donkey, and the donkey began to bray and to bellow as loud as he could; and then the Rakshas ran away quite frightened.

In the morning the Blind Man and the Deaf Man found that the floor of the house was covered with heaps of gold, and silver, and precious stones; and they made four great bundles of the treasure, and took one each, and put the other two on the donkey, and off they went, But the Rakshas was waiting some distance off to see what his father Bakshas was like by daylight; and he was very angry when he saw only a Deaf Man, and a Blind Man, and a big iron pot, and a donkey, all loaded with his gold and silver. So he ran off and fetched six of his friends to help him, and each of the six had hair a yard long, and tusks like an elephant. When the Blind Man and the Deaf Man saw them coming they went and hid the treasure in the bushes, and then they got up into a lofty betel palm and waited—the Deaf Man, because he could see, getting up first, to be furthest out of harm's way. Now the seven Rakshas were not able to reach them, and so they said, "Let us get on each other's shoulders and pull them down." So one Rakshas stooped down, and the second got on his shoulders, and the third on his, and the fourth on his, and the fifth on his, and the sixth on his, and the seventh—the one who had invited the others—was just climbing up, when the Deaf Man got frightened and caught hold of the Blind Man's arm, and as he was sitting quite at ease, not knowing that they were so close, the Blind Man was upset, and tumbled down on the neck of the seventh Rakshas. The Blind Man thought he had fallen into the branches of another tree, and stretching out his hands for something to take hold of, he seized the Rakshas' two great ears and pinched them very hard. This frightened the Rakshas, who lost his balance and fell down to the ground, upsetting the other six of his friends; the Blind Man all the while pinching harder than ever, and the Deaf Man crying out from the top of the tree—"You're all right, brother, hold on tight, I'm coming down to help you"—though he really didn't mean to do anything of the kind. Well, the noise, and the pinching, and all the confusion, so frightened the six Rakshas that they thought they had had enough of helping their friend, and so they ran away; and the seventh Rakshas, thinking that because they ran there must be great danger, shook off the Blind Man and ran away too. And then the Deaf Man came down from the tree and embraced the Blind Man, and said, "I could not have done better myself." Then the Deaf Man divided the treasure; one great heap for himself, and one little heap for the Blind Man. But the Blind Man felt his heap and then felt the other, and then, being angry at the cheat, he gave the Deaf Man a box on the ear, so tremendous that it made the Deaf Man hear. And the Deaf Man, also being angry, gave the other such a blow in the face that it made the Blind Man see. So they became good friends directly, and divided the treasure into equal shares, and went home laughing at the stupid Rakshas.

Fairy Tales; Their Origin and Meaning

From the legends of India we now go on to Persia and Arabia, to learn something about the Divs and the Peris, and the Jinns. When the ancient Persians separated from the Aryan race from which they sprang, they altered their religion as well as changed their country. They came to believe in two principal gods, Ormuzd, the spirit of goodness, who sits enthroned in the Realms of Light, with great numbers of angels around him; and Ahriman, the spirit of evil, who reigns in the Realms of Darkness and Fire, and round whose throne are the great six arch–Divs, and vast numbers of inferior Divs, or evil beings; and these two powers are always at war with each other, and are always trying to obtain the government of the world. From Ormuzd and Ahriman there came in time, according to popular fancy, the two races of the Divs and the Peris, creatures who were like mankind in some things, but who had great powers of magic; which made them visible and invisible at pleasure, enabled them to change their shapes when they pleased, and to move about on the earth or in the air. They dwelt in the land of Jinnestan, in the mountains of Kaf. These mountains were supposed to go round the earth like a ring; they were thousands of miles in height, and they were made of the precious stone called chrysolite, which is of a green colour, and this colour, so the Persian poets say, is reflected in the green which we sometimes see in the sky at sunset. In this land of Jinnestan there are many cities. The Peris have for their abode the kingdom of Shad–u–Kan, that is, of Pleasure and Delight, with its capital Juber–a–bad, or the Jewel City; and the Divs have for their dwelling Ahermambad, or Ahriman's city, in which there are enchanted castles and palaces, guarded by terrible monsters and powerful magicians. The Peris are very beautiful beings, usually represented as women with wings, and charming robes of all colours. The Divs are painted as demons of the most frightful kind. One of them, a very famous one named Berkhyas, is described as being a mountain in size, his face black, his body covered with hair, his neck like that of a dragon; two boar's tusks proceed from his mouth, his eyes are wells of blood, his hair bristles like needles, and is so thick and long that pigeons make their nests in it. Between the Peris and the Divs there was always war; but the Divs were too powerful for the Peris, and used to capture them and hang them in iron cages from the tree–tops, where their companions came and fed them with perfumes, of which the Peris are very fond, and which the Divs very much dislike, so that the smell kept the evil spirits away. Sometimes the Peris used to call in the help of men against the Divs; and in the older Persian stories there are many tales of the wonders done by these heroes who fought against the Divs. The most famous of these were called Tamuras and Rustem. Tamuras conquered so many of the evil spirits that he was called the Div–binder. He began his fights in this way. He was a great king, whose help both sides wished to get. So the Peris sent a splendid embassy to him, and so did the Divs. Tamuras did not know what to do; so he went to consult a wonderful bird, called the Simurg, who speaks all tongues, and who knows everything that has happened, or that will happen. The Simurg told him to fight for the Peris. Then the Simurg gave him three feathers from her own breast, and also the magic shield of Jan–ibn–Jan, the Suleiman or King of the Jinns, and then she carried him on her back into the country of Jinnestan, where he fought with and conquered the king of the Divs. The account of this battle is given at great length in the Persian romance poems. Then Tamuras conquered another Div, named Demrush, who lived in a gloomy cavern, where he kept in prison the Peri Merjan, or the Pearl, a beautiful fairy, whom Tamuras set free. Rustem, however, is the great hero of Persian romance, and the greatest defender of the Peris. His adventures, as told by the Persian poets, would make a very large book, so that we cannot attempt to describe them. But there are two stories of him which may be told. One night, while he lay sleeping under a rock, a Div, named Asdiv, took the form of a dragon, and came upon him suddenly. Rustem's horse, Reksh, who had magic powers, knew the Div in this disguise, and awakened his master twice, at which Rustem was angry, and tried to kill the horse for disturbing him. Reksh, however, awakened him the third time, and then Rustem saw the Div, and slew him after a fearful combat. The other story is this. There came a wild ass of enormous size, with a skin like the sun, and a black stripe along his back, and this creature got amongst the king's horses and killed them. Now the wild ass was no other than a very powerful Div, named Akvan, who haunted a particular fountain or spring. So Rustem, mounted on his horse Reksh, went to look for him there. Three days he waited, but saw nothing. On the fourth day the Div appeared, and Rustem tried to throw a noose over his head, but the Div suddenly vanished. Then he reappeared, and Rustem shot an arrow at him, but he vanished again. Rustem then turned his horse to graze, and laid himself down by the spring to sleep. This was what the cunning Akvan wanted, and while Rustem was asleep, Akvan seized him, and flew high up into the air with him. Then Rustem awoke, and the Div gave him his choice of being dropped from the sky into the sea, or upon the mountains. Rustem knew that if he fell upon the mountains he would be dashed in pieces, so he secretly chose to fall into the sea; but he did not say so to the Div. On the contrary, he pretended not to know what to do, but he said he feared the sea, because those who were drowned could not enter into Paradise. On hearing this, the Div at once dropped Rustem into the sea—which was what he wanted—and then went back to his fountain. But when he got there, he found that Rustem had got ashore, and was also at the fountain, and then they fought again and the Div was killed. After this Rustem had a son named Zohrab, about whom many wonderful things are told; and it so happened that Rustem and his son Zohrab came to fight each other without knowing one another; and Rustem was killed, and while dying he slew his son. Now all these stories mean the same thing: they are only the old Aryan Sun–myths put into another form by the poets and story–tellers: the Peris are the rays of the sun, or the morning or evening Aurora; the Divs are the black clouds of night; the hero is the sun who conquers them, and binds them in the realms of darkness; and the death of Rustem is the sunset—Zohrab, his son, being either the moon or the rising sun.

But now we must leave the Peris and the Divs, and look at the jinns, of the Arabian stories. These also dwell in the mysterious country of Jinnestan, and in the wonderful mountains of Kaf; but they likewise spread themselves all through the earth, and they specially liked to live in ruined houses, or in tombs; on the sea shore, by the banks of rivers, and at the meeting of cross–roads. Sometimes, too, they were found in deep forests, and many travellers are supposed to find them in desolate mountain places. Even to this day they are firmly believed in by Arabs, and also by people in different parts of Persia and India. In outward form, in their natural shape, they resembled the Peris and the Divs of the ancient Persians, and they were divided into good and bad: the good ones very beautiful and shining; the bad ones deformed, black, and ugly, and sometimes as big as giants. They did not, however, always appear in their own forms, for they could take the shape of any animal, especially of serpents, and cats and dogs. They were governed by chief spirits or kings; and over all, good and bad alike, there were set a succession of powerful monarchs, named Suleiman, or Solomon, seventy–two in number—the last of whom, and the greatest, Jan–ibn–Jan, is said by Arabian story–tellers to have built the pyramids of Egypt. There is an old tradition that the shield of Jan–ibn–Jan, which was a talisman of magic power, was brought from Egypt to King Solomon the Wise, the son of King David, and that it gave him power over all the tribes of the Jinns, and this is why, in the common stories about them, the Jinns are made to call upon the name of Solomon.

The Jinns, according to Arabian tradition, lived upon the earth thousands of years before man was created. They were made, the Koran says, of "the smokeless fire," that is, the hot breath of the desert wind, Simoon. But they became disobedient, and prophets were sent to warn them. They would not obey the prophets, and angels were then sent to punish them. The angels drove them out of Jinnestan into the islands of the seas, killed some, and shut some of them up in prison. Among the prisoners was a young Jinns, named Iblees, whose name means Despair; and when Adam was created, God commanded the angels and the Jinns to do him reverence, and they all obeyed but Iblees, who was then turned into a Shaitan, or devil, and became the father of all the Shaitan tribe, the mortal enemies of mankind. Since their dispersion the Jinns are not immortal; they are to live longer than man, but they must die before the general resurrection. Some of them are killed by other Jinns, some can be slain by man, and some are destroyed by shooting stars sent from heaven. When they receive a mortal wound, the fire which burns in their veins breaks forth and burns them into ashes.

Such are the Arab fancies about the Jinns. The meaning of them is clear, for the Jinns are the winds, derived plainly from the Ribhus and the Maruts of the ancient Aryan myths; and they still survive in European folk–lore in the train of Woden, or the Wild Huntsman, who sweeps at midnight over the German forests.

Some of the stories of the Jinns are to be found in the book of the Thousand and One Nights.

One of these stories is that of "the Fisherman and the Genie." A poor fisherman, you remember, goes out to cast his nets; but he draws no fish, but only, at the third cast, a vase of yellow copper, sealed with a seal of lead. He cuts open the seal, and then there issues from the vase a thick cloud of smoke, which rises to the sky, and spreads itself over land and sea. Presently the smoke gathers itself together, and becomes a solid body, taking the form of a Genie, twice as big as any of the giants; and the Genie cries out, with a terrible voice, "Solomon, Solomon, great prophet of Allah! Pardon! I will never more oppose thy will, but will obey all thy commands." At first the fisherman is very much frightened; but he grows bolder, and tells the Genie that Solomon has been dead these eighteen hundred years, to which the Genie answers that he means to kill the fisherman, and tells him why. I told you just now that the Jinns rebelled, and were punished. The Genie tells the fisherman that he is one of these rebellious spirits, that he was taken prisoner, and brought up for judgment before Solomon himself, and that Solomon confined him in the copper vase, and ordered him to be thrown into the sea, and that upon the leaden cover of the vase he put the impression of the royal seal, upon which the name of God is engraved.

When he was thrown into the sea the Genie made three vows—each in a period of a hundred years. I swore, he says, that "if any man delivered me within the first hundred years, I would make him rich, even after his death. In the second hundred years I swore that if any one set me free I would discover to him all the treasures of the earth; still no help came. In the third period, I swore to make my deliverer a most powerful monarch, to be always at his command, and to grant him every day any three requests he chose to make. Then, being still a prisoner, I swore that I would without mercy kill any man who set me free, and that the only favour I would grant him should be the manner of his death." And so the Genie proposed to kill the fisherman. Now the fisherman did not like the idea of being killed; and he and the Genie had a long discourse about it; but the Genie would have his own way, and the poor fisherman was going to be killed, when he thought of a trick he might play upon the Genie. He knew two things—first that the Jinns are obliged to answer questions put to them in the name of Allah, or God; and also that though very powerful, they are very stupid, and do not see when they are being led into a pitfall. So he said, "I consent to die; but before I choose the manner of my death, I conjure thee, by the great name of Allah, which is graven upon the seal of the prophet Solomon, the son of David, to answer me truly a question I am going to put to thee."

Then the Genie trembled, and said, "Ask, but make haste."

Now when he knew that the Genie would speak the truth, the Fisherman said, "Darest thou swear by the great name of Allah that thou really wert in that vase?"

"I swear it, by the great name of Allah," said the Genie.

But the Fisherman said he would not believe it, unless he saw it with his own eyes. Then, being too stupid to perceive the meaning of the Fisherman, the Genie fell into the trap. Immediately the form of the Genie began to change into smoke, and to spread itself as before over the shore and the sea, and then gathering itself together, it began to enter the vase, and continued to do so, with a slow and even motion, until nothing remained outside. Then, out of the vase there issued the voice of the Genie, saying, "Now, thou unbeliever, art thou convinced that I am in the vase?"

But instead of answering, the Fisherman quickly took up the leaden cover, and put it on the vase; and then he cried out, "O, Genie! it is now thy turn to ask pardon, and to choose the sort of death thou wilt have; or I will again cast thee into the sea, and I will build upon the shore a house where I will live, to warn all fishermen against a Genie so wicked as thou art."

At this the Genie was very angry. First he tried to get out of the vase; but the seal of Solomon kept him fast shut up. Then he pretended that he was but making a jest of the

Fisherman when he threatened to kill him. Then he begged and prayed to be released; but the Fisherman only mocked him. Next he promised that if set at liberty, he would make the Fisherman rich. To this the Fisherman replied by telling him a long story of how a physician who cured a king was murdered instead of being rewarded, and of how he revenged himself. And then he preached a little sermon to the Genie on the sin of ingratitude, which only caused the Genie to cry out all the more to be set free. But still the Fisherman would not consent, and so to induce him the Genie offered to tell him a story, to which the Fisherman was quite ready to listen; but the Genie said, "Dost thou think I am in the humour, shut up in this narrow prison, to tell stories? I will tell thee as many as thou wilt if thou wilt let me out." But the Fisherman only answered, "No, I will cast thee into the sea."

At last they struck a bargain, the Genie swearing by Allah that he would make the Fisherman rich, and then the Fisherman cut the seal again, and the Genie came out of the vase. The first thing he did when he got out was to kick the vase into the sea, which frightened the Fisherman, who began to beg and pray for his life. But the Genie kept his word; and took him past the city, over a mountain and over a vast plain, to a little lake between four hills, where he caught four little fish, of different colours—white, red, blue, and yellow—which the Genie bade him carry to the Sultan, who would give him more money than he had ever seen in his life. And then, the story says, he struck his foot against the ground, which opened, and he disappeared, the earth closing over him.

Another story is that of the Genie Maimoun, the son of Dimdim, who took prisoner a young Prince, and conveyed him to an enchanted palace, and changed him into the form of an ape, and the ape got on board a ship, and was carried to the country of a great Sultan, and when the Sultan heard that there was an ape who could write beautiful poems, he sent for him to the palace, and they had dinner together, and they played at chess afterwards, the ape behaving in all respects like a man, excepting that he could not speak. Then the Sultan sent for his daughter, the Queen of Beauty, to see this great wonder. But when the Queen of Beauty came into the room she was very angry with her father for showing her to a man, for the Princess was a great magician, and thus she knew that it was a man turned into an ape, and she told her father that the change had been made by a powerful Genie, the son of the daughter of Eblis. So the Sultan ordered the Queen of Beauty to disenchant the Prince, and then she should have him for her husband. On this the Queen of Beauty went to her chamber, and came back with a knife, with Hebrew characters engraved upon the blade. And then she went into the middle of the court and drew a large circle in it, and in the centre she traced several words in Arabic letters, and others in Egyptian letters. Then putting herself in the middle of the circle, she repeated several verses of the Koran. By degrees the air was darkened, as if night were coming on, and the whole world seemed to be vanishing. And in the midst of the darkness the Genie, the son of the daughter of Eblis, appeared in the shape of a huge, terrible lion, which ran at the Princess as if to devour her. But she sprang back, and plucked out a hair from her head, and then, pronouncing two or three words, she changed the hair into a sharp scythe, and with the scythe she cut the lion into two pieces through the middle. The body of the lion now vanished, and only the head remained. This changed itself into a large scorpion. The Princess changed herself into a serpent and attacked the scorpion, which then changed into an eagle, and flew away; and the serpent changed itself into a fierce black eagle, larger and more powerful and flew after it. Soon after the eagles had vanished the earth opened, and a great black and white cat appeared, mewing and crying out terribly, and with its hairs standing straight on end. A black wolf followed the cat, and attacked it. Then the cat changed into a worm, which buried itself in a pomegranate that had fallen from a tree over–hanging the tank in the court, and the pomegranate began to swell until it became as large as a gourd, which then rose into the air, rolled backwards and forwards several times, and then fell into the court and broke into a thousand pieces. The wolf now transformed itself into a cock, and ran as fast as possible, and ate up the pomegranate seeds. But one of them fell into the tank and changed into a little fish. On this the cock changed itself into a pike, darted into the water, and pursued the little fish. Then comes the end of the story, which is told by the Prince transformed into the Ape:—"They were both hid hours under water, and we knew not what was become of them, when suddenly we heard horrible cries that made us tremble. Then we saw the Princess and the Genie all on fire. They darted flames against each other with their breath, and at last came to a close attack. Then the fire increased, and all was hidden in smoke and cloud, which rose to a great height. We had other cause for terror. The Genie, breaking away from the Princess, came towards us, and blew his flames all over us." The Princess followed him; but she could not prevent the Sultan from having his beard singed and his face scorched; a spark flew into the right eye of the Ape–Prince and blinded him, and the chief of the eunuchs was killed on the spot. Then they heard the cry of "Victory! victory!" and the Princess appeared in her own form, and the Genie was reduced to a heap of ashes. Unhappily the Princess herself was also fatally hurt. If she had swallowed all the pomegranate seeds she would have conquered the Genie without harm to herself; but one seed being lost, she was obliged to fight with flames between earth and heaven, and she had only just time enough to disenchant the ape and to turn him back again into his human form, when she, too, fell to the earth, burnt to ashes.

This story is repeated in various forms in the Fairy Tales of other lands. The hair which the Princess changed into a scythe is like the sword of sharpness which appears in Scandinavian legends and in the tale of Jack the Giant Killer; the transformation of the magician reminds us of the changes of the Ogre in Puss in Boots; and the death of the Princess by fire because she failed to eat up the last of the pomegranate seeds, brings to mind the Greek myth of Persephone, who ate pomegranate seeds, and so fell into the power of Aidoneus, the God of the lower regions, and was carried down into Hades to live with him as his wife; and in many German and Russian tales are to be found incidents like those of the terrible battle between the Princess and the Genie Maimoun.

---

[7] *Old Deccan Days*. Miss and Sir Bartle Frere.

[8] *Old Deccan Days*.

CHAPTER IV. DWELLERS IN FAIRYLAND: TEUTONIC, AND SCANDINAVIAN.

Now we come to an entirely new region, in which, however, we find, under other forms, the same creatures which have already been described. From the sunny East we pass to the cold and frozen North. Here the Scandinavian countries—Norway, Sweden, and Denmark—are wonderfully rich in dwarfs, and giants, and trolls, and necks, and nisses, and other inhabitants of Fairyland; and with these we must also class the Teutonic beings of the same kind; and likewise the fairy creatures who were once supposed to dwell in our islands. The Elves of Scandinavia, with whom our own Fairies are closely allied, were a very interesting people. They were of two kinds, the White and the Black. The white elves dwelt in the air, amongst the leaves of trees, and in the long grass, and at moonlight they came out from their lurking–places, and danced merrily on the greensward, and played all manner of fantastic tricks. The black elves lived underground, and, like the dwarfs, worked in metals, and heaped up great stores of riches. When they came out amongst men they were often of a malicious turn of mind; they caused sickness or death, stole things from the houses, bewitched the cattle, and did a great deal of mischief in all ways. The good elves were not only friendly to man, but they had a great desire to get to heaven; and in the summer nights they were heard singing sweetly but sadly about themselves, and their hopes of future happiness; and there are many stories of their having spoken to mortals, to ask what hope or chance they had of salvation. This feeling is believed to have come from the sympathy felt by the first converts to Christianity with their heathen forefathers, whose spirits were supposed by them to wander about, in the air or in the woods, or to sigh within their graves, waiting for the day of judgment. In one place there is a story that on a hill at Garun people used to hear very beautiful music. This was played by the elves, or hill folk, and any one who had a fiddle, and went there, and promised the elves that they should be saved, was taught in a moment how to play; but those who mocked them, and told them they could never be saved, used to hear the poor elves, inside the hill, breaking their fairy fiddles into pieces, and weeping very sadly. There is a particular tune they play, called the Elf–King's tune, which, the story–tellers say, some good fiddlers know very well, but never venture to play, because everybody who hears it is obliged to dance, and to go on dancing till somebody comes behind the musician and cuts the fiddle–strings; and out of this tradition we have the story of the Pied Piper of Hamelin. Some of the underground elves come up into the houses built above their dwellings, and are fond of playing tricks upon servants; but they like only those who are clean in their habits, and they do not like even these to laugh at them. There is a story of a servant–girl whom the elves liked very much, because she used to carry all dirt and foul water away from the house, and so they invited her to an Elf Wedding, at which they made her a present of some chips, which she put into her pocket. But when the bridegroom and the bride were coming home there was a straw lying in their way. The bridegroom got over it; but the bride stumbled, and fell upon her face. At this the servant–girl laughed out loud, and then all the elves vanished, but she found that the chips they had given her were pieces of pure gold. At Odensee another servant was not so fortunate. She was very dirty, and would not clean the cow–house for them; so they killed all the cows, and took the girl and set her up on the top of a hay–rick. Then they removed from the cow–house into a meadow on the farm; and some people say that they were seen going there in little coaches, their king riding first, in a coach much handsomer than the rest. Amongst the Danes there is another kind of elves—the Moon Folk. The man is like an old man with a low–crowned hat upon his head; the woman is very beautiful in front, but behind she is hollow, like a dough–trough, and she has a sort of harp on which she plays, and lures young men with it, and then kills them. The man is also an evil being, for if any one comes near him he opens his mouth and breathes upon them, and his breath causes sickness. It is easy to see what this tradition means: it is the damp marsh wind, laden with foul and dangerous odours; and the woman's harp is the wind playing across the marsh rushes at nightfall. Sometimes these elves take the shape of trees, which brings back to mind the Greek fairy tales of nymphs who live and die with the trees to which they are united.

These Scandinavian elves were like beings of the same kind who were once supposed to live in England, Ireland, and Scotland, and who are still believed in by some country people. Scattered about in the traditions which have been brought together at different times are many stories of these fanciful beings. One story is of some children of a green colour who were found in Suffolk, and who said they had lived in a country where all the people were of a green colour, and where they saw no sun, but had a light like the glow which comes after sunset. They said, also, that while tending their flocks they wandered into a great cavern, and heard the sound of delightful bells, which they followed, and so came out upon the upper world of the earth. There is a Yorkshire legend of a peasant coming home by night, and hearing the voices of people singing. The noise came from a hill–side, where there was a door, and inside was a great company of little people, feasting. One of them offered the man a cup, out of which he poured the liquor, and then ran off with the cup, and got safe away. A similar story is told also of a place in Gloucestershire, and of another in Cumberland, where the cup is called "the Luck of Edenhall," as the owners of it are to be always prosperous, so long as the cup remains unbroken. Such stories as this are common in the countries of the North of Europe, and show the connection between our Elf–land and theirs.

The Pixies, or the Devonshire fairies, are just like the northern elves. The popular idea of them is that they are small creatures—pigmies—dressed in green, and are fond of dancing. Some of them live in the mines, where they show the miners the richest veins of metal just like the German dwarfs; others live on the moors, or under the shelter of rocks; others take up their abode in houses, and, like the Danish and Swedish elves, are very cross if the maids do not keep the places clean and tidy others, like the will–o'–the–wisps, lead travellers astray, and then laugh at them. The Pixies are said to be very fond of pure water. There is a story of two servant–maids at Tavistock who used to leave them a bucket of water, into which the Pixies dropped silver pennies. Once it was forgotten, and the Pixies came up into the girls' bedroom, and made a noise about the neglect. One girl got up and went to put the water in its usual place, but the other said she would not stir out of bed to please all the fairies in Devonshire. The girl who filled the water–bucket found a handful of silver pennies in it next morning, and she heard the Pixies debating what to do with the other girl. At last they said they would give her a lame leg for seven years, and that then they would cure her by striking her leg with a herb growing on Dartmoor. So next day Molly found herself lame, and kept so for seven years, when, as she was picking mushrooms on Dartmoor, a strange–looking boy started up, struck her leg with a plant he held in his hand, and sent her home sound again. There is another story of the Pixies which is very beautiful. An old woman near Tavistock had in her garden a fine bed of tulips, of which the Pixies became very fond, and might be heard at midnight singing their babes to rest amongst them; and as the old woman would never let any of the tulips be plucked, the Pixies had them all to themselves, and made them smell like the rose, and bloom more beautifully than any flowers in the place. Well, the old woman died, and the tulip–bed was pulled up and a parsley–bed made in its place. But the Pixies blighted it, and nothing grew in it; but they kept the grave of the old woman quite green, never suffered a weed to grow upon it, and in spring–time they always spangled it with wild–flowers.

All over the country, in the far North as in the South, we find traces of elfin beings like the Pixies—the fairies of the common traditions and of the poets—some such fairies as Shakspeare describes for us in several of his plays, especially in "Midsummer–Night's Dream," "The Merry Wives of Windsor," "The Tempest," and "Romeo and Juliet"—fairies who gambol sportively.

> "On hill, in dale, forest, or mead,
> By paved fountain, or by rushing brook,
> Or by the beached margent of the sea,
> To dance their ringlets to the whistling wind."

But the Fairy tribe were not the only graceful elves described by the poets. The Germans had their Kobolds, and the Scotch their Brownies, and the English had their Boggarts and Robin Goodfellow and Lubberkin—all of them beings of the same description: house and farm spirits, who liked to live amongst men, and who sometimes did hard, rough work out of good–nature, and sometimes were spiteful and mischievous, especially to those who teased them, or spoke of them disrespectfully, or tried to see them when they did not wish to be seen. To the same family belongs the Danish Nis, a house spirit of whom many curious legends are related. Robin Goodfellow was the original of Shakspeare's Puck: his frolics are related for us in "The Midsummer Night's Dream," where a hairy says to him—

Fairy Tales; Their Origin and Meaning

> "You are that shrewd and knavish sprite
> Called Robin Goodfellow. Are you not he
> That frights the maidens of the villagery,
> Skims milk, and sometimes labours in the quern,
> And bootless makes the breathless housewife churn;
> And sometimes makes the drink to bear no harm,
> Misleads night wanderers, laughing at their harm?
> Those that Hob—Goblin call you, and sweet Puck;
> You do their work, and they shall have good luck."

In the "Jests of Robin Goodfellow," first printed in Queen Elizabeth's reign, the tricks which this creature is said to have played are told in plenty. Here is one of them:—Robin went as fiddler to a wedding. When the candles came he blew them out, and giving the men boxes on the ears he set them fighting. He kissed the prettiest girls, and pinched the ugly ones, till he made them scratch one another like cats. When the posset was brought he turned himself into a bear, frightened them all away, and had it all to himself.

The Boggart was another form of Robin Goodfellow. Stories of him are to be found amongst Yorkshire legends, as of a creature— always invisible—who played tricks upon the people in the houses in which he lived: shaking the bed—curtains, rattling the doors, whistling through the keyholes, snatching away the bread—and—butter from the children, playing pranks upon the servants, and doing all kinds of mischief. There is a story of a Yorkshire boggart who teased the family so much that the farmer made up his mind to leave the house. So he packed up his goods and began to move off. Then a neighbour came up, and said, "So, Georgey, you're leaving the old house?" "Yes," said the farmer, "the boggart torments us so that we must go." Then a voice came out of a churn, saying, "Ay, ay, Georgey, *we're* flitting, ye see." "Oh!" cried the poor farmer, "if thou'rt with us we'll go back again;" and he went back.—Mr. Tennyson puts this story into his poem of "Walking to the Mail."

> "His house, they say,
> Was haunted with a jolly ghost, that shook
> The curtains, whined in lobbies, tapt at doors,
> And rummaged like a rat: no servant stayed:
> The farmer, vext, packs up his beds and chairs,
> And all his household stuff, and with his boy

Betwixt his knees, his wife upon the tilt,
Sets out, and meets a friend who hails him, 'What!
You're flitting!' 'Yes, we're flitting,' says the ghost
(For they had packed the thing among the beds).
'Oh, well,' says he, 'you flitting with us, too;
Jack, turn the horses' heads and home again.'"

The same story is told in Denmark, of a Nis—which is the same as an English boggart, a Scotch brownie, and a German kobold— who troubled a man very much, so that he took away his goods to a new house. All but the last load had gone, and when they came for that, the Nis popped his head out of a tub, and said to the man, "We're moving, you see."

The Brownies, though mischievous, like the Boggarts, were more helpful, for they did a good deal of house–work; and would bake, and brew, and wash, and sweep, but they would never let themselves be seen; or if any one did manage to see them, or tried to do so, they went away. There are stories of this kind about them in English folk–lore, in Scotch, Welsh, in the Isle of Man, and in Germany, where they were called Kobolds. One Kobold, of whom many accounts are given, lived in the castle of Hudemuhler, in Luneberg, and used to talk with the people of the house, and with visitors, and ate and drank at table, just like Leander in the story of "The Invisible Prince;" and he used also to scour the pots and pans, wash the dishes, and clean the tubs, and he was useful, too, in the stable, where he curried the horses, and made them quite fat and smooth. In return for this he had a room to himself, where he made a straw–plaited chair, and had a little round table, and a bed and bedstead, and, where he expected every day to find a dish of sweetened milk, with bread crumbs; and if he did not get served in time, or if anything went wrong, he used to beat the servants with a stick. This Kobold was named Heinzelman, and in Grimm's collection of folklore there is a long history of him drawn up by the minister of the parish. Another Kobold, named Hodeken, who lived with the Bishop of Hildesheim, was usually of a kind and obliging turn of mind, but he revenged himself on those who offended him. A scullion in the bishop's kitchen flung dirt upon him, and Hodeken found him fast asleep and strangled him, and put him in the pot on the fire. Then the head cook scolded Hodeken, who in revenge squeezed toads all over the meat that was being cooked for the bishop, and then took the cook himself and tumbled him over the drawbridge into the moat. Then the bishop got angry, and took bell, and book, and candle, and banished Hodeken by the form of exorcism provided for evil spirits.

Fairy Tales; Their Origin and Meaning

Now there are a great many other kinds of creatures in the Wonderland of all European countries; but I must not stop to tell you about them or we shall never have done. But there is one little story of the Danish Nis—who answers to the German Kobold—which I may tell you, because it is like the story of Hodeken which you have just read, and shows that the creatures were of the same kind. There was a Nis in Jutland who was very much teased by a mischievous boy. When the Nis had done his work he sat down to have his supper, and he found that the boy had been playing tricks with his porridge and made it unpleasant. So he made up his mind to be revenged, and he did it in this way. The boy slept with a servant–man in the loft. The Nis went up to them and took off the bed–clothes. Then, looking at the little boy lying beside the tall man, he said, "Long and short don't match," and he took the boy by the legs and pulled him down to the man's legs. This was not to his mind, however, so he went to the head of the bed and looked at them, Then said the Nis— "Short and long don't match," and he pulled the boy up again; and so he went on all through the night, up and down, down and up, till the boy was punished enough. Another Nis in Jutland went with a boy to steal corn for his master's horses. The Nis was moderate, but the boy was covetous, and said, "Oh, take more; we can rest now and then!" "Rest," said the Nis, "rest! what is rest?" "Do what I tell you," replied the boy; "take more, and we shall find rest when we get out of this." So they took more corn, and when they had got nearly home the boy said, "Here now is rest;" and so they sat down on a hill–side. "If I had known," said the Nis, as they were sitting there, "if I had known that rest was so good I'd have carried off all that was in the barn."

Now we must leave out much more that might be said, and many stories that might be told, about elves, and fairies, and nixes, or water spirits, and swan maidens who become women when they lay aside their swan dresses to bathe; and mermaids and seal maidens, who used to live in the islands of the North seas. And we must leave out also a number of curious Scotch tales and accounts of Welsh fairies, and stories about the good people of the Irish legends, and the Leprechaun, a little old man who mends shoes, and who gives you as much gold as you want if you hold him tight enough; and there are wonderful fairy legends of Brittany, and some of Spain and Italy, and a great many Russian and Slavonic tales which are well worth telling, if we only had room. For the same reason we must omit the fairy tales of ancient Greece, some of which are told so beautifully by Mr. Kingsley in his book about the Heroes; and we must also pass by the legends of King Arthur, and of romances of the same kind which you may read at length in Mr. Ludlow's "Popular Epics of the Middle Ages;" and the wonderful tales from the Norse which are told by Dr. Dasent, and in Mr. Morris's noble poem of "Sigurd the Volsung."

Fairy Tales; Their Origin and Meaning

But before we leave this part of Wonderland we must say something about some kinds of beings who have not yet been mentioned—the Scandinavian Giants and Trolls, and the German Dwarfs. The Trolls—some of whom were Giants and some Dwarfs— were a very curious people. They lived inside hills or mounds of earth, sometimes alone, and sometimes in great numbers. Inside these hills, according to the stories of the common folk, are fine houses made of gold and crystal, full of gold and jewels, which the Trolls amuse themselves by counting. They marry and have families; they bake and brew, and live just like human beings; and they do not object, sometimes, to come out and talk to men and women whom they happen to meet on the road. They are described as being friendly, and quite ready to help those to whom they take a fancy—lending them useful or precious things out of the hill treasures, and giving them rich gifts. But, to balance this, they are very mischievous and thievish, and sometimes they carry off women and children. They dislike noise. This, so the old stories say, is because the god Thor used to fling his hammer at them; and since he left off doing that the Trolls have suffered a great deal from the ringing of church bells, which they very much dislike. There are many stories about this. At a place called Ebeltoft the Trolls used to come and steal food out of the pantries. The people consulted a Saint as to what they were to do, and he told them to hang up a bell in the church steeple, which they did, and then the Trolls went away. There is another story of the same kind. A Troll lived near the town of Kund, in Sweden, but was driven away by the church bells. Then he went over to the island of Funen and lived in peace. But he meant to be revenged on the people of Kund, and he tried to take his revenge in this way: He met a man from Kund—a stranger, who did not know him—and asked the man to take a letter into the town and to throw it into the churchyard, but he was not to take it out of his pocket until he got there. The man received the letter, but forgot the message, until he sat down in a meadow to rest, and then he took out the letter to look at it. When he did so, a drop of water fell from under the seal, then a little stream, and then quite a torrent, till all the valley was flooded, and the man had hard work to escape. The Troll had shut up a lake in the letter, and with this he meant to drown the people of Kund.

Some of the Trolls are very stupid, and there are many stories as to how they have been outwitted. One of them is very droll. A farmer ploughed a hill–side field. Out came a Troll and said, "What do you mean by ploughing up the roof of my house?" Then the farmer, being frightened, begged his pardon, but said it was a pity such a fine piece of land should lie idle. The Troll agreed to this, and then they struck a bargain that the farmer should till the land and that each of them should share the crops. One year the

Troll was to have, for his share, what grew above ground, and the next year what grew underground. So in the first year the farmer sowed carrots, and the Troll had the tops; and the next year the farmer sowed wheat, and the Troll had the roots; and the story says he was very well content.

We can give only one more story of the Trolls. They have power over human beings until their names are found out, and when the Troll's name is mentioned his power goes from him. One day St. Olaf, a very great Saint, was thinking how he could build a very large church without any money, and he didn't quite see his way to it. Then a Giant Troll met him and they chatted together, and St. Olaf mentioned his difficulty. So the Troll said he would build the church, within a year, on condition that if it was done in the time he should have for his reward the sun, and the moon, or St. Olaf himself. The church was to be so big that seven priests could say mass at seven altars in it without hearing each other; and it was all to be built of flint stone and to be richly carved. When the time was nearly up the church was finished, all but the top of the spire; and St. Olaf was in sad trouble about his promise. So he walked out into a wood to think, and there he heard the Troll's wife hushing her child inside a hill, and saying to it, "To-morrow, Wind and Weather, your father, will come home in the morning, and bring with him the sun and the moon, or St. Olaf himself." Then St. Olaf knew what to do. He went home, and there was the church, all ready except the very top of the weather-cock, and the Troll was just putting the finishing-touch to that. Then St. Olaf called out to him, "Oh! ho! Wind and Weather, you have set the spire crooked!" And then, with a great noise, the Troll fell down from the steeple and broke into pieces, and every piece was a flint-stone.

The same thing is told in the German story of Rumpelstiltskin. A maiden is ordered by a King to spin a roomful of straw into gold, or else she is to die. A Dwarf appears, she promises him her necklace, and he does the task for her. Next day she has to spin a larger roomful of straw into gold. She gives the Dwarf the ring off her finger, and he does this task also. Next day she is set to work at a larger room, and then, when the Dwarf comes, she has nothing to give him. Then he says, "If you become Queen, give me your first-born child." Now the girl is only a miller's daughter, and thinks she never can be Queen, so she makes the promise, and the Dwarf spins the straw into gold. But she does become Queen, for the King marries her because of the gold; and she forgets the Dwarf, and is very happy, especially when her little baby comes. Directly it is born the Dwarf appears also, and claims the child, because it was promised to him. The Queen offers him anything he likes besides; but he will have that, and that only. Then she cries and prays, and the Dwarf says that if she can tell him his name she may keep the baby; and he feels quite safe in saying this, because nobody knows his name, only himself. So the Queen calls him by all kinds of strange names, but none of them is the right one. Then she begs for three days to find out the name, and sends people everywhere to see if they can hear it. But all of them come back, unable to find any name that is likely, excepting one, who says, "I have not found a name, but as I came to a high mountain near the edge of a forest, where the foxes and the hares say 'good–night' to each other, I saw a little house, and before the door a fire was burning, and round the fire a little man was dancing on one leg, and singing:—

"To–day I stew, and then I'll bake,
To–morrow shall I the Queen's child take.
How glad I am that nobody knows
That my name is Rumpelstiltskin."

Then the Dwarf came again, and the Queen said to him, "Is your name Hans?" "No," said the Dwarf, with an ugly leer, and he held out his hands for the baby. "Is it Conrade?" asked the Queen. "No," cried the Dwarf, "give me the child." "Then," said the Queen, "is it Rumpelstiltskin?" "A witch has told you that!" cried the Dwarf; and then he stamped his right foot so hard upon the ground that it sank quite in, and he could not draw it out again. Then he took hold of his left leg with both his hands and pulled so hard that his right leg came off, and he hopped away howling, and nobody ever saw him again.

The Giant in the story of St. Olaf, as we have seen, was a rather stupid giant, and easily tricked; and indeed most of the giants seem to have been dull people, from the great Greek Kyklops, Polyphemos the One–Eyed, downwards to the, ogres in Puss in Boots, and Jack and the Bean Stalk, and the giants in Jack the Giant Killer. The old northern giants were no wiser. There was one in the island of Rugen, a very mighty giant, named Balderich. He wanted to go from his island, dry–footed, to the mainland. So he got a great apron made, and filled it with earth, and set off to make a causeway from Rugen to Pomerania. But there was a hole in the apron, and the clay that fell out formed a chain of nine hills. The giant stopped the hole and went on, but another hole tore in the apron, and thirteen more hills fell out. Then he got to the sea–side, and poured the rest of the load into the water; but it didn't quite reach the mainland, which made giant Balderich so angry that he fell down and died; and so his work has never been finished. But a giant maiden thought she would try to make another causeway from the mainland to an island, so that she might not wet her slippers in going over. So she filled her apron with sand, and ran down to the sea–side. But a hole came in the apron, and the sand which ran out formed a hill at Sagard. The giant maiden said, "Ah! now my mother will scold me!" Then she stopped the hole with her hand and ran on again. But the giant mother looked over the wood, and cried, "You nasty child! what are you about? Come here, and you'll get a good whipping." The daughter in a fright let go her apron, and all the sand ran out, and made the barren hills near Litzow, which the white and brown dwarfs took for their dwelling–place.

There are many other stories of the same kind. One of them tells of a Troll Giant who wanted to punish a farmer; so he filled one of his gloves with sand, and poured it out over the farmer's house, which it quite covered up; and with what was left in the fingers he made a row of little sand hillocks to mark the spot.

The Giants had their day, and died out, and their places were taken by the Dwarfs. Some of the most wonderful dwarf stories are those which are told in the island of Rugen, in the Baltic Sea. These stories are of three kinds of dwarfs: the White, and the Brown, and the Black, who live in the sand–hills. The white dwarfs, in the spring and summer, dance and frolic all their time in sunshine and starlight, and climb up into the flowers and trees, and sit amongst the leaves and blossoms, and sometimes they take the form of bright little birds, or white doves, or butterflies, and are very kind to good people. In the winter, when the snow falls, they go underground, and spend their time in making the most beautiful ornaments of silver and gold. The brown dwarfs arc stronger and rougher than the white; they wear little brown coats and brown caps, and when they dance—which they are fond of doing—they wear little glass shoes; and in dress and appearance they are very handsome. Their disposition is good, with one exception—that they carry off children into their underground dwellings; and those who go there have to serve them for fifty years. They can change themselves into any shape, and can go through key–holes, so that they enter any house they please, and sometimes they bring gifts for the children, like the good Santa Klaus in the German stories; but they also play sad tricks, and frighten people with bad dreams. Like the white dwarfs, the brown ones work in gold and silver, and the gifts they bring are of their own workmanship. The black dwarfs are very bad people, and are ugly in looks and malicious in temper; they never dance or sing, but keep underground, or, when they come up, they sit in the elder–trees, and screech horribly like owls, or mew like cats. They, too, are great metal–workers, especially in steel; and in old days they used to make arms and armour for the gods and heroes: shirts of mail as fine as cobwebs, yet so strong that no sword could go through them; and swords that would bend like rushes, and yet were as hard as diamonds, and would cut through any helmet, however thick.

So long as they keep their caps on their heads the dwarfs are invisible; but if any one can get possession of a dwarf's cap he can see them, and becomes their master. This is the foundation of one of the best of the dwarf stories—the story of John Dietrich, who went out to the sandhills at Ramfin, in the isle of Rugen, on the eve of St. John, a very, very long time ago, and managed to strike off the cap from the head of one of the brown dwarfs, and went down with them into their underground dwelling–place. This was quite a little town, where the rooms were decorated with diamonds and rubies, and the dwarf people had gold and silver and crystal table–services, and there were artificial birds that flew about like real ones, and the most beautiful flowers and fruits; and the dwarfs, who were thousands in number, had great feasts, where the tables, ready spread, came up through the floor, and cleared themselves away at the ringing of a bell, and left the rooms free for dancing to the strains of the loveliest music. And in the city there were fields and gardens, and lakes and rivers; and instead of the sun and the moon to give light, there were large carbuncles and diamonds which supplied all that was wanted. John Dietrich, who was very well treated, liked it very much, all but one thing—which was that the servants who waited upon the dwarfs were earth children, whom they had stolen and carried underground; and amongst them was Elizabeth Krabbin, once a playmate of his own, and who was a lovely girl, with clear blue eyes and ringlets of fair hair. John Dietrich of course fell in love with Elizabeth, and determined to get her out of the dwarf people's hands, and with her all the earth children they held captive. And when he had been ten years underground, and he and Elizabeth were grown up, he demanded leave to depart, and to take Elizabeth. But the dwarfs, though they could not hinder him from going, would not let her go, and no threats or entreaties could move them. Then John Dietrich remembered that the little people cannot bear an evil smell; and one day he happened to break a large stone, out of which jumped a toad, which gave him power to do what he pleased with the dwarfs, for the sight or smell of a toad causes them pain beyond all bearing. So he sent for the chiefs of the dwarfs, and bade them let Elizabeth go. But they refused; and then he went and fetched the toad. Then the story goes on in this way:—

"He was hardly come within a hundred paces of them when they all fell to the ground as if struck with a thunderbolt, and began to howl and whimper, and to writhe as if suffering

64

the most excruciating pain. The dwarfs stretched out their hands, and cried, 'Have mercy, have mercy! we feel that you have a toad, and there is no escape for us. Take the odious beast away, and we will do all you require.' He let them kneel a few seconds longer, and then took the toad away. They then stood up, and felt no more pain. John let all depart but the six chief persons, to whom he said, 'This night, between twelve and one, Elizabeth and I will depart, Load for me three waggons with gold, silver, and precious stones. I might, you know, take all that is in the hill; but I will be merciful. Further, you must put into two waggons all the furniture of my chamber (which was covered with emeralds and other precious stones, and in the ceiling was a diamond as big as a nine–pin bowl), and get ready for me the handsomest travelling carriage that is in the hill, with six black horses. Moreover, you must set at liberty all the servants who have been so long here that on earth they would be twenty years old and upwards, and you must give them as much silver and gold as will make them rich for life; and you must make a law that no one shall be kept here longer than his twentieth year.'

"The six took the oath, and went away quite melancholy, and John buried his toad deep in the ground. The little people laboured hard and prepared everything, and at midnight John and Elizabeth, and their companions, and all their treasures, were drawn up out of the hill. It was then one o'clock, and it was midsummer—the very time that, twelve years before, John had gone down into the hill. Music sounded around them, and they saw the glass hill open, and the rays of the light of heaven shine on them after so many years; and when they got out they saw the first streaks of dawn already in the East. Crowds of the underground people were around them, busied about the waggons. John bid them a last farewell, waved his brown cap in the air, and then flung it among them. And at the same moment he ceased to see them; he beheld nothing but a green hill, and the well–known bushes and fields, and heard the church clock of Ramfin strike two. When all was still, save a few larks, who were tuning their morning song, they all fell upon their knees and worshipped God, resolving henceforth to lead a pious and Christian life." And then John married Elizabeth, and was made a count, and built several churches, and presented to them some of the precious cups and plates made by the underground people, and kept his own and Elizabeth's glass shoes, in memory of what had befallen them in their youth. "And they were all taken away," the story says, "in the time of the great Charles the Twelfth of Sweden, when the Russians came on the island, and the Cossacks plundered even the churches, and took away everything."

Now there is much more to be told about the dwarfs, if only we had space—how there were thousands of them in German lands, in the Saxon mines, and the Black Forest, and the Harz mountains and in other places, and in Switzerland, and indeed everywhere almost—how they gave gifts to good men, and borrowed of them, and paid honestly; how they punished those who injured them; how they moved about from country to country; how they helped great kings and nobles, and showed themselves to wandering travellers and to simple country folk. But all this must be left for you to read for yourselves in Grimm's stories, and in the legends of northern lands, and in many collections of ancient poems, and romances, and popular tales. And in these, and in other books which deal with such subjects, you will find out that all these dwellers in Wonderland, and the tales that are told about them, and the stories of the gods and heroes, all come from the one source of which we read something in the first chapter—the tradition's of the ancient Aryan people, from whom all of us have sprung—and how they all mean the same things; the conflict between light and darkness, the succession of day and night, the changes of the seasons, the blue and bright summer skies, the rain–clouds, the storm–winds, the thunder and the lightning, and all the varied and infinite forms of Nature in her moods of calm and storm, peace and tempest, brightness and gloom, sweet and pleasant and hopeful life and stern and cold death, which causes all brightness to fade and moulder away.

CHAPTER V. DWELLERS IN FAIRYLAND: WEST HIGHLAND STORIES.

In a very delightful book which has already been mentioned, Campbell's "Popular Tales of the West Highlands," there are many curious stories of fairy folk and other creatures of the like kind, described in the traditions of the west of Scotland, and which are still believed in by many of the country people. There are Brownies, for instance, the farm spirits. One of these, so the story goes, inhabited the island of Inch, and looked after the cattle of the Mac Dougalls; but if the dairymaid neglected to leave a portion of milk for him at night, one of the cattle would be sure to fall over the rocks. Another kind of Brownie, called the Bocan, haunted a place called Moran, opposite the Isle of Skye, and protected the family of the Macdonalds of Moran, but was very savage to other people, whom he beat or killed. At last Big John, the son of M'Leod of Raasay, went and fought the creature in the dark, and tucked him under his arm, to carry him to the nearest light and see what he was like. But the Brownies hate to be seen, and this one begged hard to be let off, promising that he would never come back. So Big John let him off, and he flew away singing:—

"Far from me is the hill of Ben Hederin;
 Far from me is the Pass of Murmuring;"

and the common story says that the tune is still remembered and sung by the people of that country. It is also told of a farmer, named Callum Mohr MacIntosh, near Loch Traig, in Lochaber, that he had a fight with a Bocan, and in the fight he lost a charmed handkerchief. When he went back to get it again, he found the Bocan rubbing the handkerchief hard on a flat stone, and the Bocan said, "It is well for you that you are back, for if I had rubbed a hole in this you were a dead man." This Bocan became very friendly with MacIntosh, and used to bring him peats for fire in the deep winter snows; and when MacIntosh moved to another farm, and left a hogshead of hides behind him by accident, the Bocan carried it to his new house next morning, over paths that only a goat could have crossed.

Another creature of the same kind is a mischievous spirit, a Goblin or Brownie, who is called in the Manx language, the Glashan, and who appears under various names in Highland stories: sometimes as a hairy man, and sometimes as a water– horse turned into a man. He usually attacks lonely women, who outwit him, and throw hot peats or scalding water at him, and then he flies off howling. One feature is common to the stories about him. He asks the woman what her name is, and she always replies "Myself." So when the companions of the Glashan ask who burned or scalded him, he says "Myself," and then they laugh at him. This answer marks the connection between these tales and those of other countries. Polyphemos asks Odysseus his name, and is told that it is Outis, or "Nobody." So when Odysseus blinds Polyphemos, and the other Kyklopes ask the monster who did it, he says, "Nobody did it." There is a Slavonian story, also, in which a cunning smith puts out the eyes of the Devil, and says that his name is Issi, "myself;" and when the tortured demon is asked who hurt him, he says, "Issi did it;" and then his companions ridicule him.

Among other Highland fairy monsters are the water–horses (like the Scandinavian and Teutonic Kelpies) and the water–bulls, which inhabit lonely lochs. The water–bulls are described as being friendly to man; the water–horses are dangerous—when men get upon their backs they are carried off and drowned. Sometimes the water–horse takes the shape of a man. Here is a story of this kind from the island of Islay: There was a farmer who had a great many cattle. Once a strange—looking bull—calf was born amongst them, and an old woman who saw it knew it for a water—bull, and ordered it to be kept in a house by itself for seven years, and fed on the milk of three cows. When the time was up, a servant—maid went to watch the cattle graze on the side of a loch. In a little while a man came to her and asked her to dress or comb his hair. So he laid his head upon her knees, and she began to arrange his hair. Presently she got a great fright, for amongst the hair she found a great quantity of water—weed; and she knew that it was a transformed water—horse. Like a brave girl she did not cry out, but went on dressing the man's hair until he fell asleep. Then she slid her apron off her knees, and ran home as fast as she could, and when she got nearly home, the creature was pursuing her in the shape of a horse. Then the old woman cried out to them to open the door of the wild bull's house, and out sprang the bull and rushed at the horse, and they never stopped fighting until they drove each other out into the sea. "Next day," says the story, "the body of the bull was found on the shore all torn and spoilt, but the horse was never more seen at all."

Sometimes the water—spirit appears in the shape of a great bird, which the West Highlanders called the Boobrie, who has a long neck, great webbed feet with tremendous claws, a powerful bill hooked like an eagle's, and a voice like the roar of an angry bull. The lochs, according to popular fancy, are also inhabited by water—spirits. In Sutherlandshire this kind of creature is called the Fuath; there are, Mr. Campbell says, males and females; they have web—feet, yellow hair, green dresses, tails, manes, and no noses; they marry human beings, are killed by light, are hurt by steel weapons, and in crossing a stream they become restless. These spirits resemble mermen and mermaids, and are also like the Kelpies, and they have also been somehow confused with the kind of spirit known in Ireland as the Banshee. Many stories are told of them. A shepherd found one, an old woman seemingly crippled, at the edge of a bog. He offered to carry her over on his back. In going over, he saw that she was webfooted; so he threw her down, and ran for his life. By the side of Loch Middle a woman saw one—"about three years ago," she told the narrator—she sat on a stone, quiet, and dressed in green silk, the sleeves of the dress curiously puffed from the wrists to the shoulder; her hair was yellow, like ripe corn; but on a nearer view, she had no nose. A man at Tubernan made a bet that he would seize the Fuath or Kelpie who haunted the loch at Moulin na Fouah. So he took a brown right—sided maned horse, and a brown black—muzzled dog, and with the help of the dog he captured the Fuath, and tied her on the horse behind him. She was very fierce, but he pinned her down with an awl and a needle. Crossing the burn or brook near Loch Migdal she grew very restless, and the man stuck the awl and the needle into her with great force. Then she cried, "Pierce me with the awl, but keep that slender hair–like slave (the needle) out of me." When the man reached an inn at Inveran, he called his friends to come out and look at the Fuath. They came out with lights, and when the light fell upon her she dropped off the horse, and fell to the earth like a small lump of jelly.

The Fairies of the West Highlands in some degree resembled the Scandinavian Dwarfs. They milked the deer; they lived underground, and worked at trades, especially metal–working and weaving. They had hammers and anvils, but had to steal wool and to borrow looms; and they had great hoards of treasure hidden in their dwelling places. Sometimes they helped the people whom they liked, but at other times they were spiteful and evil minded; and according to tradition all over the Highlands, they enticed men and women into their dwellings in the hills, and kept them there sometimes for years, always dancing without stopping. There are many stories of this kind; and there are also many about the fondness of the Fairies for carrying off human children, and leaving Imps of their own in their places— these Imps being generally old men disguised as children. Some of these tales are very curious, and are like others that are found amongst the folk–lore of Celtic peoples elsewhere. Here is the substance of one told in Islay:—

Years ago there lived in Crossbrig a smith named MacEachern, who had an only son, about fourteen; a strong, healthy, cheerful boy. All of a sudden he fell ill, took to his bed, and moped for days, getting thin, and odd–looking, and yellow, and wasting away fast, so that they thought he must die. Now a "wise" old man, who knew about Fairies, came to see the smith at work, and the poor man told him all about his trouble. The old man said, "It is not your son you have got; the boy has been carried off by the Dacorie Sith (the Fairies), and they have left a sibhreach (changeling) in his place." Then the old man told him what to do. "Take as many egg–shells as you can get, go with them into the room, spread them out before him, then draw water with them, carrying them two and two in your hands as if they were a great weight, and when they are full, range them round the fire." The smith did as he was told; and he had not been long at work before there came from the bed a great shout of laughter, and the supposed boy cried out, "I am eight hundred years old, and I never saw the like of *that* before." Then the smith knew that it was not his own son. The wise man advised him again. "Your son," he said, "is in a green round hill where the Fairies live; get rid of this creature, and then go and look for him." So the smith lit a fire in front of the bed. "What is that for?" asked the supposed boy. "You will see presently," said the smith; and then he took him and threw him into the middle of it; and the sibhreach gave an awful yell, and flew up through the roof, where a hole was left to let the smoke out. Now the old man said that on a certain night the green round hill, where the Fairies kept the smith's boy, would be open. The father was to take a Bible, a dirk, and a crowing cock, and go there. He would hear singing, and dancing, and much merriment, but he was to go boldly in. The Bible would protect him against the Fairies, and he was to stick the dirk into the threshold, to prevent the hill closing upon him. Then he would see a grand room, and there, working at a forge, he would find his own son; and when the Fairies questioned him he was to say that he had come for his boy, and would not go away without him. So the smith went, and did what the old man told him. He heard the music, found the hill open, went in, stuck the dirk in the threshold, carried the Bible on his breast, and took the cock in his hand. Then the Fairies angrily asked what he wanted, and he said, "I want my son whom I see down there, and I will not go without him." Upon this the whole company of the Fairies gave a loud laugh, which woke up the cock, and he leaped on the smith's shoulders, clapped his wings, and crowed lustily. Then the Fairies took the smith and his son, put them out of the hill, flung the dirk after them, and the hill–side closed up again. For a year and a day after he got home the boy never did any work, and scarcely spoke a word; but at last one day sitting by his father, and seeing him finish a sword for the chieftain, he suddenly said, "That's not the way to do it," and he took the tools, and fashioned a sword the like of which was never seen in that country before; and from that day he worked and lived as usual.

Here is another story. A woman was going through a wild glen in Strath Carron, in Sutherland—the Glen Garaig—carrying her infant child wrapped in her plaid. Below the path, overhung with trees, ran a very deep ravine, called Glen Odhar, or the dun glen. The child, not a year old, suddenly spoke, and said:—

"Many a dun hummel cow,
  With a calf below her,
  Have I seen milking
  In that dun glen yonder,
  Without dog, without man,
  Without woman, without gillie,
  But one man; and he hoary."

Then the woman knew that it was a fairy changeling she was carrying, and she flung down the child and the plaid, and ran home, where her own baby lay smiling in the cradle.

A tailor went to a farm–house to work, and just as he was going in, somebody put into his hands a child of a month old, which a little lady dressed in green seemed to be waiting to receive. The tailor ran home and gave the child to his wife. When he got back to the farm–house he found the farmer's child crying and yelping, and disturbing everybody. It was a fairy changeling which the nurse had taken in, meaning to give the farmer's own child to the fairy in exchange; but nobody knew this but the tailor. When they were all gone out he began to talk to the child. "Hae ye your pipes?" said the Tailor. "They're below my head," said the Changeling. "Play me a spring," said the Tailor. Out sprang the little man and played the bagpipes round the room. Then there was a noise outside, and the Elf said, "Its my folk wanting me," and away he went up the chimney; and then they fetched back the farmer's child from the tailor's house.

One more story: it is told by the Sutherland–shire folk. A small farmer had a boy who was so cross that nothing could be done with him. One day the farmer and his wife went out, and put the child to bed in the kitchen; and they bid the farm lad to go and look at it now and then, and to thrash out the straw in the barn. The lad went to look at the child, and the Child said to him in a sharp voice, "What are you going to do?" "Thrash out a pickle of straw," said the Lad, "lie still and don't grin, like a good bairn." But the little Imp of out of bed, and said, "Go east, Donald, and when ye come to the big brae (or brow of the hill), rap three times, and when *they* come, say ye are seeking Johnnie's flail." Donald did so, and out came a little fairy man, and gave him a flail. Then Johnnie took the flail, thrashed away at the straw, finished it, sent the flail back, and went to bed again. When the parents came back, Donald told them all about it; and so they took the Imp out of the cradle, put it in a basket, and set the basket on the fire. No sooner did the creature feel the fire than he vanished up the chimney. Then there was a low crying noise at the door, and when they opened it, a pretty little lad, whom the mother knew to be her own, stood shivering outside.

A few notes about West Highland giants must end this account of wonder creatures in this region. There was a giant in Glen Eiti, a terrible being, who comes into a wild strange story, too long to be told here. He is described as having one hand only, coming out of the middle of his chest, one leg coming out of his haunch, and one eye in the middle of his face. And in the same story there is another giant called the Fachan, and the story says, "Ugly was the make of the Fachan; there was one hand out of the ridge of his chest,

71

and one tuft out of the top of his head; it were easier to take a mountain from the root than to bend that tuft." Usually, the Highland giants were not such dreadful creatures as this. Like giants in all stories, they were very stupid, and were easily outwitted by cunning men. "The Gaelic giants (Mr. Campbell says)[9] are very like those of Norse and German tales, but they are much nearer to real men than the giants of Germany and Scandinavia and Greece and Rome, who are almost, if not quite, equal to the gods. Their world is generally, though not always, underground; it has castles, and parks, and pasture, and all that is found above on the earth. Gold, and silver, and copper abound in the giants' land, jewels are seldom mentioned, but cattle, and horses, and spoil of dresses, and arms, and armour, combs, and basins, apples, shields, bows, spears, and horses are all to be gained by a fight with the giants. Still, now and then a giant does some feat quite beyond the power of man, such as a giant in Barra, who fished up a hero, boat and all, with his fishing–rod, from a rock and threw him over his head, as little boys do 'cuddies' from the pier end. So the giants may be degraded gods, after all." In the story of Connal, told by Kenneth MacLennan of Pool Ewe, there is a giant who was beaten by the hero of the tale. Connal was the son of King Cruachan, of Eirinn, and he set out on his adventures. He met a giant who had a great treasure of silver and gold, in a cave at the bottom of a rock, and the giant used to promise a bag of gold to anybody who would allow himself to be let down in a creel or basket, and send some of it up. Many people were lost in trying it, for when the giant had let them down, and they had filled the creel, the giant used to draw up the creel of gold, and then he would not let it down again, and so those who had gone down for it were left to perish in the deep cavern. Now Connal agreed to go down, and the giant served him in the same way that he had done the rest, and Connal was left in the cave among the dead men and the gold. Now the giant could not get anybody else to go down, and as he wanted more gold, he let his own son down in the creel, and gave him the sword of light, so that he might see his way before him. When the young giant got into the cave, Connal took the sword of light very quickly, and cut off the young giant's head, Then Connal put gold into the bottom of the creel, and got in himself, and covered himself over with gold, and gave a pull at the rope, and the giant drew up the creel, and when he did not see his son, he threw the creel over the back of his head; and Connal took the sword of light, and cut off the giant's head, and went away home with the sword and the gold.

There was a King of Lochlin, who had three daughters, and three giants stole them, and carried them down under the earth; and a wise man told the King that the only way to get them back was to make a ship that would sail over land or sea. So the King said that anybody who would make such a ship should marry his eldest daughter. There was a widow who had three sons, and the eldest of them said he would go into the forest and cut wood, and make the ship; and his mother gave him a large bannock (oat cake), and away he went. Then a Fairy came out of the river, and asked for a bit of the bannock, but he would not give her a morsel; so he began cutting the wood, but as fast as he cut them down, the trees grew up again, and he went home sorrowful. Then the next brother did the same, and he failed also. Then the youngest brother went, and he took a little bannock, instead of a big one, and the Fairy came again, and he gave her a share of the bannock; and she told him to meet her there in a year and a day, and the ship should be ready. And it was ready, and the youngest son sailed away in it. Then he came to a man who was drinking up a river; and the youngest son hired him for a servant. After a time, he found a man who was eating a whole ox, and he hired him too. Then he saw another man, with his ear to the earth, and he said he was hearing the grass grow; so he hired him also. Then they got to a great cave, and the last man listened, and said it was where the three giants kept the King's three daughters, and they went down into the cave, and up to the house of the biggest giant. "Ha! ha!" said the Giant, "you are seeking the King's daughter, but thou wilt not have her, unless thou hast a man who will drink as much water as I." Then the river–drinker set to work, and so did the giant, and before the man was half satisfied, the giant burst. Then they went to where the second giant was. "Ho! ho!" said the Giant, "thou art seeking the King's daughter, but thou wilt not get her, if thou hast not a man who will eat as much flesh as I." Then the ox–eater began, and so did the giant; but before the man was half satisfied, the giant burst. Then they went on to the third Giant; and the Giant said to the youngest son that he should have the King's daughter if he would stay with him for a year and a day as a slave. Then they sent up the King's three daughters, and the three men out of the cave; and the youngest son stayed with the giant for a year and a day. When the time was up the youngest son said, "Now I am going." Then the Giant said, "I have an eagle that will take thee up;" and he put him on the eagle's back, and fifteen oxen for the eagle to eat on her way up; but before the eagle had got half way up she had eaten all the oxen, and came back again. So the youngest son had to stay with the giant for another year and a day. When the time was up, the Giant put him on the eagle again, and thirty oxen to last her for food; but before she got to the top she ate them all, and so went back again; and the young man had to stay another year and a day with the giant. At the end of the third year and a day, the Giant put him on the eagle's back a third time, and gave her three score of oxen to eat; and just when they got to the mouth of the cave, where the earth began, all the oxen were eaten, and the eagle was going back again. But the young man cut a piece out of his own thigh, and gave it to the eagle, and with one spring she was on the surface of the earth. Then the Eagle said to him, "Any hard lot that comes to thee, whistle, and I will be at thy side." Now the youngest son went to the town where the King of Lochlin lived with the daughters he had got back from the giants; and he hired himself to work at blowing the bellows for a smith. And the King's oldest daughter ordered the smith to make her a golden crown like that she had when she was with the giant, or she would cut off his head. The bellows–blower said he would do it. So the smith gave him the gold, and he shut himself up, and broke the gold into splinters, and threw it out of the window, and people picked it up. Then he whistled for the Eagle, and she came, and he ordered her to fetch the gold crown that belonged to the biggest giant; and the Eagle fetched it, and the smith took it to the King's daughter, who was quite satisfied. Then the King's second daughter wanted a silver crown like that she had when she was with the second giant; and the King's youngest daughter wanted a copper crown, like that she had when she was with the third Giant; and the Eagle fetched them both for the young man, and the smith took them to the King's daughters. Then the King asked the smith how he did all this; and the smith said it was his bellows–blower who did it. So the King sent a coach and four horses for the bellows–blower, and the servants took him, all dirty as he was, and threw him into the coach like a dog. But on the way he called the eagle, who took him out of the coach, and filled it with stones, and when the King opened the door, the stones fell out upon him, and nearly killed him; and then, the story says, "There was catching of the horse gillies, and hanging them for giving such an affront to the King." Then the King sent a second time, and these messengers also were very rude to the bellows–blower, so he made the eagle fill the coach with dirt, which fell about the King's ears, and the second set of servants were punished. The third time the King sent his trusty servant, who was very civil, and asked the bellows–blower to wash himself, and he did so, and the eagle brought a gold and silver dress that had belonged to the biggest giant, and when the King opened the coach door there was sitting inside the very finest man he ever saw. And the young man told the King all that had happened, and they gave him the King's eldest daughter for his wife, and the wedding lasted twenty days and twenty nights.

One story more, of how a Giant was outwitted by a maiden. It is told in the island of Islay. There was a widow, who had three daughters, who went out to seek their fortunes. The two elder ones did not want the youngest, and they tied her in turns to a rock, a peat–stack, and a tree, but she got loose and came after them. They got to the house of a Giant, and had leave to stop for the night, and were put to bed with the Giant's daughters. The Giant came home and said, "The smell of strange girls is here," and he ordered his gillie to kill them; and the gillie was to know them from the Giant's daughters by these having twists of amber beads round their necks, and the others having twists of horse–hair. Now Maol o Chliobain, the youngest of the widow's daughters, heard this, and she changed the necklaces, and so the gillie came and killed the Giant's daughters, and Maol o Chliobain took the golden cloth that was on the bed, and ran away with her sisters. But the cloth was an enchanted cloth, and it cried out to the Giant, who pursued them till they came to a river, and then Maol plucked out a hair of her head, and made a bridge of it; but the Giant could not get over; so he called out to Maol, "And when wilt thou come again?" "I will come when my business brings me," she said; and then he went home again. They got to a farmer's house, and told him their history. Said the Farmer, who had three sons, "I will give my eldest son to thy eldest sister; get for me the fine comb of gold and the coarse comb of silver that the Giant has." So she went and fetched the combs, and the Giant followed her till they came to the river, which the Giant could not get over; so he went back again. Then the farmer said he would marry his second son to the second sister, if Maol would get him the sword of light that the Giant had. So she went to the Giant's house, and got up into a tree that was over the well; and when the Giant's gillie came to draw water, she came down and pushed him into the well, and carried away the sword of light that he had with him. Then the Giant followed her again, and again the river stopped him; and he went back. Now the farmer said he would give his youngest son to Maol o Chliobain herself, if she would bring him the buck the Giant had. So she went, but when she had caught the buck, the Giant caught her. And he said, "Thou least killed my three daughters, and stolen my combs of gold and silver; what wouldst thou do to me if I had done as much harm to thee as thou to me?" She said, "I would make thee burst thyself with milk porridge, I would then put thee in a sack, I would hang thee to the roof–tree, I would set fire under thee, and I would lay on thee with clubs till thou shouldst fall as a faggot of withered sticks on the floor." So the Giant made milk porridge and forced her to drink it, and she lay down as if she were dead. Then the Giant put her in a sack, and hung her to the roof tree, and he went away to the forest to get wood to burn her, and he left his old mother to watch till he came back. When the Giant was gone Maol o Chliobain began to cry out, "I am in the light; I am in the city of gold." "Wilt thou let me in?" said the Giant's mother. "I will not let thee in," said Maol o Chliobain. Then the Giant's mother let the sack down, and Maol o Chliobain got out, and she put into the sack the Giant's mother, and the cat, and the calf, and the cream–dish; and then she took the buck and went away. When the Giant came back he began beating the sack with clubs, and his Mother cried out, "Tis I myself that am in it." "I know that thyself is in it," said the Giant, and he laid on all the harder. Then the sack fell down like a bundle of withered sticks, and the Giant found that he had killed his mother. So he knew that Maol o Chliobain had played him a trick, and he went after her, and got up to her just as she leaped over the river. "Thou art over there, Maol o Chliobain" said the Giant. "I am over," she said. "Thou killedst my three bald brown daughters?" "I killed them, though it is hard for thee." "Thou stolest my golden comb, and my silver comb?" "I stole them." "Thou killedst my bald rough–skinned gillie?" "I killed him." "Thou stolest my glaive (sword) of light?" "I stole it." "Thou killedst my mother?" "I killed her, though it is hard for thee." "Thou stolest my buck?" "I stole it." "When wilt thou come again?" "I will come when my business brings me." "If thou wert over here, and I yonder," said the Giant, "what wouldst thou do to follow me?" "I would kneel down," she said, "and I would drink till I should dry the river." Then the poor foolish Giant knelt down, and he drank till he burst; and then Maol o Chliobain went off with the buck and married the youngest son of the farmer.

---

[9] *Popular Tales of the West Highlands*, vol. i., Introduction, p. c.

CHAPTER VI. CONCLUSION: SOME POPULAR TALES EXPLAINED.

This brings us towards the end—that is, to show how some of our own familiar stories connect themselves with the old Aryan myths, and also to show something of what they mean. There are four stories which we know best—Cinderella, and Little Red Riding Hood, and Jack the Giant Killer, and Jack and the Bean Stalk—and the last two of these belong especially to English fairy lore.

Now about the story of Cinderella. We saw something of her in the first chapter: How she is Ushas, the Dawn Maiden of the Aryans, and the Aurora of the Greeks; and how the Prince is the Sun, ever seeking to make the Dawn his bride, and how the envious stepmother and sisters are the Clouds and the Night, which strive to keep the Dawn and the Sun apart. The story of Little Red Riding Hood, as we call her, or Little Red Cap, as she is called in the German tales, also comes from the same source, and refers to the Sun and the Night. You all know the story so well that I need not repeat it: how Little Red Riding Hood goes with nice cakes and a pat of butter to her poor old grandmother; how she meets on the way with a wolf, and gets into talk with him, and tells him where she is going; how the wolf runs off to the cottage to get there first, and eats up the poor grandmother, and puts on her clothes, and lies down in her bed; how Little Red Riding hood, knowing nothing of what the wicked wolf has done, comes to the cottage, and gets ready to go to bed to her grandmother, and how the story goes on in this way:—

"Grandmother," (says Little Red Riding Hood), "what great arms you have got!"

"That is to hug you the better, my dear."

"Grandmother, what, great ears you have got!"

That is to hear you the better, my dear."

"Grandmother, what great eyes you have got!"

"That is to see you the better, my dear."

"Grandmother, what a great mouth you have got!"

"That is to eat you up!" cried the wicked wolf; and then he leaped out of bed, and fell upon poor Little Red Riding Hood, and ate her up in a moment.

This is the English version of the story, and here it stops; but in the German story there is another ending to it. After the wolf has eaten up Little Red Riding Hood he lies down in bed again, and begins to snore very loudly. A huntsman, who is going by, thinks it is the old grandmother snoring, and he says, "How loudly the old woman snores; I must see if she wants anything." So he stepped into the cottage, and when he came to the bed he found the wolf lying in it. "What! do I find you here, you old sinner?" cried the huntsman; and then, taking aim with his gun, he shot the wolf quite dead.

Now this ending helps us to see the full meaning of the story. One of the fancies in the most ancient Aryan or Hindu stories was that there was a great dragon that was trying to devour the sun, and to prevent him from shining upon the earth and filling it with brightness and life and beauty, and that Indra, the sun–god, killed the dragon. Now this is the meaning of Little Red Riding Hood, as it is told in our nursery tales. Little Red Riding Hood is the evening sun, which is always described as red or golden; the old Grandmother is the earth, to whom the rays of the sun bring warmth and comfort. The

Wolf—which is a well-known figure for the clouds and blackness of night—is the dragon in another form; first he devours the grandmother, that is, he wraps the earth in thick clouds, which the evening sun is not strong enough to pierce through. Then, with the darkness of night he swallows up the evening sun itself, and all is dark and desolate. Then, as in the German tale, the night–thunder and the storm winds are represented by the loud snoring of the Wolf; and then the Huntsman, the morning sun, comes in all his strength and majesty, and chases away the night-clouds and kills the Wolf, and revives old Grandmother Earth, and brings Little Red Riding Hood to life again. Or another explanation may be that the Wolf is the dark and dreary winter that kills the earth with frost, and hides the sun with fog and mist; and then the Spring comes, with the huntsman, and drives winter down to his ice–caves again, and brings the Earth and the Sun back to life. Thus, you see, how closely the most ancient myth is preserved in the nursery tale, and how full of beautiful and hopeful meaning this is when we come to understand it. The same idea is repeated in another story, that of "The Sleeping Beauty in the Wood," where the Maiden is the Morning Dawn, and the young Prince, who awakens her with a kiss, is the Sun which comes to release her from the long sleep of wintry night.

The germ of the story of "Jack and the Bean Stalk" is to be found in old Hindu tales, in which the beans are used as the symbols of abundance, or as meaning the moon, and in which the white cow is the clay and the black cow is the night. There is also a Russian story in which a bean falls upon the ground and grows up to the sky, and an old man, meaning the sun, climbs up by it to heaven, and sees everything. This comes very near the story of Jack, who sells his cow for a handful of beans, and his mother scatters them in the garden, and throws her apron over her head and weeps, thus figuring the Night and the Rain; and, shielded by the night and watered by the rain, the bean grows up to the sky, and Jack climbs to the Ogre's land, and carries off the bags of gold, and the wonderful hen that lays a golden egg every day, and the golden harp that plays tunes by itself. It is also possible that the bean–stalk which grows from earth to heaven is a remembrance, brought by the Norsemen, of the great tree, Ygdrassil, which, in the Norse mythology, has its roots in hell and its top in heaven; and the evil Demons dwell in the roots, and the earth is placed in the middle, and the Gods live in the branches. And there is another explanation given, namely, that "the Ogre in the land above the skies, who was once the All–father, possessed three treasures: a harp which played of itself enchanting music, bags of gold and diamonds, and a hen which daily laid a golden egg. The harp is the wind, the bags are the clouds dropping the sparkling rain, and the golden egg laid every day by the red hen is the dawn–produced sun."[10] Thus, in the story of "Jack and the Bean Stalk" we find repeated the same idea which appears in Northern and Eastern fairy tales, and in Greek legends; and so we are carried back to the ancient Hindu traditions, and to the myths of Nature−worship amongst the old Aryan race.

It is the same with the story of "Jack the Giant Killer," which also has its connection with the legends of various countries and all ages, and has also its inner meaning, drawn from the beliefs and traditions of the ancient past. There is no need to tell you the adventures of Jack the Giant Killer; how he kills the Cornish giant Cormoran by tumbling him into a pit and striking him on the head with a pick−axe; how he strangles Giant Blunderbore and his friend by throwing ropes over their heads and drawing the nooses fast until they are choked; how he cheats the Welsh giant by putting a block of wood into his own bed for the giant to hammer at and by slipping the hasty−pudding into a leathern bag, and then ripping it up, to induce the giant to do the same with his own stomach, which he does, and so kills himself; or how he frightens the giant with three heads, and so gets the coat of darkness, the cap of knowledge, the shoes of swiftness, and the sword of sharpness, and uses these to escape from other and more terrible masters, and to kill them; and gets the duke's daughter for his wife, and lives honoured and happy ever after.

Now Jack the Giant Killer is really one of the very oldest and most widely−known characters in Wonderland. He is the hero who, in all countries and ages, fights with monsters and overcomes them; like Indra, the ancient Hindu sun−god, whose thunderbolts slew the demons of drought in the far East; or Perseus, who, in Greek story, delivers the maiden from the sea−monster; or Odysseus, who tricks the giant Polyphemus, and causes him to throw himself into the sea; or Thor, whose hammer beats down the frost−giants of the North. The gifts bestowed upon Jack are found in Tartar stories, in Hindu tales, in German legends, and in the fables of Scandinavia. The cloak is the cloud cloak of Alberich, king of the old Teutonic dwarfs, the cap is found in many tales of Fairyland, the shoes are like the sandals of Hermes, the sword is like Arthur's Excalibur, or like the sword forged for Sigurd, or that which was made by the horse−smith, Velent, the original of Wayland Smith, of old English legends. This sword was so sharp, that when Velent smote his adversary it seemed only as if cold water had glided down him. "Shake thyself," said Velent; and he shook himself, and fell dead in two halves. The trick which Jack played upon the Welsh giant is related in the legend of the god Thor and the giant Skrimner. The giant laid himself down to sleep under an oak, and Thor struck him with his mighty hammer. "Hath a leaf fallen upon me from the tree?" said the giant. Thor struck him again on the forehead. "What is the matter," said

Skrimner, "hath an acorn fallen upon my head?" A third time Thor struck his tremendous blow. Skrimner rubbed his cheek and said, "Methinks some moss has fallen upon my face." The giant had done what Jack did: he put a great rock upon the place where Thor supposed him to be sleeping, and the rock received all the blows. The whole story probably means no more than this: Jack the Giant Killer is the Wind and the Light which disperses the mists and overthrows the cloud giants; and popular fancy, ages ago, dressed him out as a person combating real giants of flesh and blood, just as in all ages and all countries the forces of nature have taken personal shape, and have given us these tales of miraculous gifts, of great deeds done, and of monsters destroyed by men with the courage and the strength of heroes.

Now our task is done. We have seen that the Fairy Stories came from Asia, where they were made, ages and ages ago, by a people who spread themselves over our Western world, and formed the nations which dwell in it, and brought their myths and legends with them; and we have seen, too, how the ancient meanings are still to be found in the tales that are put now into children's books, and are told by nurses at the fireside. And we have seen something of the lessons they teach us, and which are taught by all the famous tales of Wonderland; lessons of kindness to the feeble and the old, and to birds, and beasts, and all dumb creatures; lessons of courtesy, courage, and truth–speaking; and above all, the first and noblest lesson believed in by those who were the founders of our race, that God is very near to us, and is about us always; and that now, as in all times, He helps and comforts those who live good and honest lives, and do whatever duty lies clear before them.

---

[10] Baring–Gould, *Myths of the Middle Ages.*

CPSIA information can be obtained
at www.ICGtesting.com
Printed in the USA
BVHW010930240921
617281BV00011B/281

9 781162 662329